T0328453

Cambridge Elements ≡

Elements in Race, Ethnicity, and Politics
edited by
Megan Ming Francis
University of Washington

RACIAL ORDER, RACIALIZED RESPONSES

Interminority Politics in a Diverse Nation

Efrén O. Pérez
UCLA

E. Enya Kuo
Yale University

CAMBRIDGE
UNIVERSITY PRESS

University Printing House, Cambridge CB2 8BS, United Kingdom

One Liberty Plaza, 20th Floor, New York, NY 10006, USA

477 Williamstown Road, Port Melbourne, VIC 3207, Australia

314–321, 3rd Floor, Plot 3, Splendor Forum, Jasola District Centre, New Delhi – 110025, India

103 Penang Road, #05–06/07, Visioncrest Commercial, Singapore 238467

Cambridge University Press is part of the University of Cambridge.

It furthers the University's mission by disseminating knowledge in the pursuit of education, learning, and research at the highest international levels of excellence.

www.cambridge.org
Information on this title: www.cambridge.org/9781108958530
DOI: 10.1017/9781108953757

© Efrén O. Pérez and E. Enya Kuo 2021

First published 2021

A catalogue record for this publication is available from the British Library.

ISBN 978-1-108-95853-0 Paperback
ISSN 2633-0423 (online)
ISSN 2633-0415 (print)

Cambridge University Press has no responsibility for the persistence or accuracy of URLs for external or third-party internet websites referred to in this publication and does not guarantee that any content on such websites is, or will remain, accurate or appropriate.

Racial Order, Racialized Responses

Interminority Politics in a Diverse Nation

Elements in Race, Ethnicity, and Politics

DOI: 10.1017/9781108953757
First published online: September 2021

Efrén O. Pérez
UCLA

E. Enya Kuo
Yale University

Author for correspondence: Efrén O. Pérez, perezeo@ucla.edu

Abstract: America's racial sands are quickly shifting, with parallel growth in theories to explain how varied groups respond, politically, to demographic changes. This Element develops a unified framework to predict when, why, and how racial groups react defensively toward others. America's racial groups can be arrayed along two dimensions: how *American* and how *superior* are they considered? This Element claims that location along these axes motivates political reactions to out-groups. Using original survey data and experiments, this Element reveals the acute sensitivity that people of color have to their social station and how it animates political responses to racial diversity.

Keywords: interminority politics, racial hierarchy, experiments, Black politics, Asian American politics

ISBNs: 9781108958530 (PB), 9781108953757 (OC)
ISSNs: 2633-0423 (online), 2633-0415 (print)

Contents

1 Introduction: Diversity of People, Diversity of Explanations

> The U.S. has confronted each racially defined minority with a unique form of despotism and degradation. The examples are familiar . . . blacks were subjected to racial slavery, Mexicans were invaded and colonized, and Asians faced exclusion.
>
> Omi and Winant (1986: 1)

Despite writing these words more than three decades ago, Michael Omi and Howard Winant's observation remains as illuminating as ever. America's people of color are still systematically marginalized in distinctly unique ways, limiting each group's access to full and equal rights at various levels of government (e.g., Acuña 1981; Carter 2019; Junn 2007; Kim 2003; Kuo, Malhotra, and Mo 2017; Masuoka and Junn 2013; McClain and Johnson Carew 2017; Pantoja, Ramirez, and Segura 2001; Pérez 2021; Sidanius and Petrocik 2001). Indeed, as the scholar Salvador Vidal-Ortíz has remarked, people of color are "similarly disadvantaged, even if their disadvantages are based on different variables" (Vidal-Ortíz 2008: 1037).

The scientific response to this plethora of experiences could not be more breathtaking. Numerous scholars have rushed to firmly grasp the implications for racialized exclusion on each minority group's politics, with researchers plowing entire new subfields that are closely attuned to the unique nuances of each community of color. These separate caches of literature have accumulated into robust and elegant explanations for the political behavior of African Americans (e.g., Dawson 1994; Gay 2006; Greer 2013; Philpot 2017; Tate 1991; Watts Smith 2014; White and Laird 2020), Asian Americans (Junn and Masuoka 2008; Kuo et al. 2017; Lien, Conway, and Wong 2004; Wong et al. 2011), Latinos (Abrajano 2010; Abrajano and Alvarez 2010; Beltrán 2010; García 2012; Garcia Bedolla 2005; Pérez 2015a, 2015b; Silber Mohamed 2017; Zepeda-Millán 2017), and several other non-White groups (e.g., Lajevardi 2020; Nagel 1996; Oskooii 2016).

Insofar as an expansive understanding of US minority politics is concerned, this explosion in specialized research agendas is a boon for political science. We now know, more than we did before, how racial exclusion bears on the political outlooks of variegated communities (cf. McClain and Johnson Carew 2017). Yet a comprehensive understanding of US minority politics – that is, knowledge produced by drawing on the same framework across multiple groups – remains glaringly rare. As America's sea of racial diversity continues to churn, our discipline still generally shuns unified, theoretical frameworks that explain interminority politics in every sense of this word.

We think this is a mistake and one we hope to begin rectifying in the coming pages. As scholars of US racial and ethnic politics (REP), we fully recognize that no two groups have been systematically oppressed in the same exact way. But as political psychologists, we also believe that from these thickets of unique experiences, we can draw out the kernels for a unified framework that places diverse racial and ethnic groups on a common plane. The point of doing so is not to flatten group histories or obliterate their contemporary realities (e.g., Beltrán 2010; Dawson 2011; García 2012; Nagel 1996; Omi and Winant 1986; Takaki 1989). Rather, it is to facilitate REP scholars' deeper appreciation for how different channels of racial exclusion modulate people of color's reactions to each other (cf. Kim 1999, 2003). Our goal in this Element, then, is to develop a broad theoretical explanation for when, why, and how racial and ethnic minority groups respond, politically, to one another. In striving for this object-ive, we urge REP scholars to view interminority relations, not as characterized by conflict or cooperation, but as a field where these general postures depend, in large part, on the interplay between psychological dispositions and social position within America's hierarchy of groups.

2 Racial Subordination and Interminority Politics

What drives the political reactions that minority groups express toward each other? We argue that the political response of people of color to other non-Whites is conditioned by their own unique position in America's racial hier-archy. Since our country's inception, intergroup relations have been organized around a stable order where Whites are perched atop and people of color are arrayed below in terms of prestige and power (Masuoka and Junn 2013; Omi and Winant 1986; Sidanius et al. 1997). Despite this arrangement, however, the renowned political scientist, Michael Dawson, has noted how this "American racial order is a phenomenon with which many researchers are loathe to deal" (Dawson 2000: 344).

"Many researchers," of course, does not imply all scholars. Several analysts, many of them social and political psychologists, have robustly emphasized the role of structural considerations in configuring the web of interrelationships between America's racial and ethnic groups, what is formally dubbed a racial hierarchy (cf. Carter and Pérez 2016; Junn 2007; King 2000; Kim 2003; Marx 1998; Masuoka and Junn 2013; Sidanius et al. 1997; Sidanius and Petrocik 2001; Sidanius and Pratto 1999). With some useful revisions here and there (Kim 2003; Masuoka and Junn 2013; Xu and Lee 2013), this powerful lens reveals that higher (lower) ranks along America's racial hierarchy can propel the political behavior of specific groups and their members. Thus, we learn that African Americans' lower position in the racial order – a position sustained by deep, ongoing, and systemic discrimination and devaluation – has stimulated the development of a strong sense of collective identity that is chronically accessible and politically influential (e.g., Block 2011; Brown and Davis 2002; Dawson 1994, 2001; Tate 2000; White and Laird 2020; White, Laird, and Allen 2014). At the top of the hierarchy, research shows that members of the predominant group – Whites – are lashing out socially and politically against the perceived encroachment of minorities into domains that Whites consider "rightfully" theirs (e.g., Abrajano and Hajnal 2015; Craig and Richeson 2014, 2018; Danbold and Huo 2015; Jardina 2019; Lowery, Knowles, and Unzueta 2007; Pérez, Deichert, and Engelhardt 2019).

But what about other racial groups, such as Asian Americans (the fastest-growing non-White group in the United States) and Latinos (the largest non-White segment of the US population)? In a hierarchy where all of the action is restricted to a very narrow corridor running from *superior* to *inferior*, scholars have felt forced to place both of these communities on the lower end of this top-down arrangement. But as any political scientist is likely to admit, even good theories like this one leak at the joints.

Take the case of Asian Americans. While it is indisputable that Asians are a group that continues to experience racial discrimination and subjugation (Kim 2003; Xu and Lee 2013), what *is* debatable is the degree to which they are neatly nestled, conceptually, right alongside African Americans. For instance, consider the label, *honorary Whites*, which some scholars have pinned on Asian Americans (Bonilla-Silva 2004; Jiménez and Horowitz 2013). The notion here is that inasmuch as Asian Americans are relegated to an *inferior* status, their collective experience is replete with exceptions to this otherwise general rule. In the aggregate, Asian Americans earn more than their Black, Latino, and even White counterparts (Jiménez 2017; Pérez 2021). Moreover, Asian Americans are less likely than African Americans and Latinos to live in dense, urban settings (Jiménez and Horowitz 2013). When compared to African Americans, Asian Americans also display higher intermarriage rates with Whites, suggesting that some in the dominant group consider Asian individuals (typically women) more suitable domestic partners (Lee and Bean 2010).

Many of these empirical trends have crystallized into widely available and broadly endorsed stereotypes about Asian American individuals. For example, Asian Americans are often stereotyped as a *model minority* on the basis of their allegedly high level of innate intelligence and strong cultural values emphasizing education (Lee and Zhou 2015; Sakamoto, Goyette, and Kim, 2009; Sue and Okazaki, 1990; Tseng, Chao, and Padmawidjaja, 2007). Yet these individual-level generalizations overlook the structural roots of the contemporary Asian American population – a highly competitive system of immigrant admissions that generates the self-selection of highly educated and professionally skilled immigrants from primarily East Asian countries (Junn 2007; Ngai 2004). In our view, the current rendering of America's racial order fails to capture this complexity of the Asian American experience.

Latinos similarly represent a round peg in a square hole. They are deemed comparable to African Americans on many fronts. Like Black Americans, many Latinos are brutalized by law enforcement agencies that include not only police departments but also border enforcement units (Cortez 2017, 2020). And like African Americans, many Latinos are also held in low regard by society, with astoundingly excessive high school dropout rates, relatively low college enrollments, and stiff incarceration rates used as evidence of this deserved status (Flores et al. 2017; Mancilla-Martínez 2018). However, unlike African Americans – a community with deep roots in the United States – some Latinos (particularly those descended from immigrants) are gradually incorporating themselves into mainstream life, as evidenced by higher inter-marriage rates with Whites, higher suburbanization rates, and increased political visibility in Congress (Sears 2015; Sears and Savalei 2006; see also Alba and Nee 2003; Citrin et al. 2007; Jiménez 2010; Telles and Ortiz 2008; Telles and Sue 2019). The eminent political scientist David Sears characterizes many of these trends as underscoring America's "Black Exceptionalism": the sobering notion that the US more quickly absorbs some people of color, yet continues to widely and systematically marginalize many African Americans within the body politic. In our view, this further reiterates the need to revise our understanding of how, exactly, racial and ethnic groups are arrayed in a more nuanced and complicated field of intergroup relations (cf. Kim 1999).

2.1 Two Axes of Subordination to Grasp Interminority Politics

Our discussion up to this point suggests that perhaps – just perhaps – the conventional view of racial hierarchy as falling along a *superior-inferior* dimension is in need of revision, particularly if we wish to develop a more unified framework that accommodates various group's experiences, while making crisper and more precise predictions about their politics in intergroup settings. But how to accomplish this?

While the options here are several (e.g., Blumer 1958; Bobo and Hutchings 1996; Bonilla-Silva 2004; Masuoka and Junn 2013), we hitch our conceptual wagon to Linda Zou and Sapna Cheryan (2017): two social psychologists who have invested considerable effort in developing a parsimonious, two-dimensional framework that captures the persistence of America's racial hierarchy, while doing greater justice to the multiplicity of experiences that various non-White groups undergo in America (cf. Blumer 1958; Bobo and Hutchings

1996; Kim 2003). Although this framework is fundamentally psychological in origin and scope, we will expand its reach here to politics – and in particular, to the nature of *intergroup* politics among people of color.

Fully aware of the inherent tensions in a strictly top-down hierarchy, Zou and Cheryan (2017) have developed what they call the Racial Position Model (RPM). The main embers for their thinking are the insights of political scientist Claire Jean Kim (1999, 2003). Kim's theory of racial triangulation has taught many political scientists that Asian Americans are structurally subordinated in between White Americans and African Americans as a "higher status" but "foreign" group. For Kim (1999, 2003), this triangulation is but one way through which White supremacy is enshrined and reinforced in the United States.

Building on this insight, Zou and Cheryan's RPM stipulates that Whites are still the most valorized group in the United States. However, major shifts in rankings come from people of color and their respective stations in relation to Whites and each other. To this end, non-Whites are reconceptualized as falling along two major axes of subordination. The first of these is the familiar *superior-inferior* dimension that has shaped many political scientists' thinking (e.g., Blumer 1958; Bobo and Hutchings 1996; Carter and Pérez 2016; Masuoka and Carter 2013; Sidanius et al. 1997). Here, Whites are construed as the most *superior* group – that is, the group with the most cachet or social prestige. Punching right below Whites are Asian Americans: a racial group considered to be higher-status than Blacks and Latinos, but not as socially esteemed as Whites. This liminal station expressly acknowledges Asians' more complicated status within America's racial order (Kim 2003; Xu and Lee 2013).

The second axis of subordination, in turn, involves the ranking of groups in terms of how *American* or *foreign* they are considered to be. Once again, Whites occupy the most advantaged position along this corridor as the most *American* group, which is evidenced by their regular efforts to limit others' entry into this highly valorized category (cf. Danbold and Huo 2015; Pérez et al. 2019). But what about people of color? Here, the jockeying for position along this axis reflects the complex and unique ways in which different racial minority groups experience their subordination. For example, African Americans are positioned here as a relatively more *American* group than Asians and Latinos, who contain substantial numbers of immigrants in their ranks. That is, in comparison to Asian Americans and Latinos – two groups which are regularly construed as "foreign intruders" – Black individuals are considered *relatively more American* than this pair of communities (Carter 2019).

This revised hierarchy is visually represented in Figure 1, which we adapt from Zou and Cheryan (2017). The simple two-by-two reveals some interesting

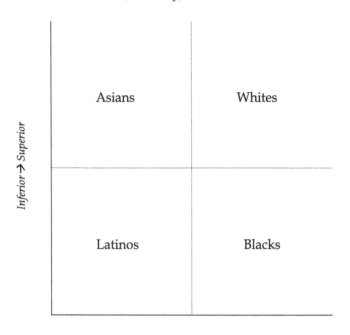

Foreign →American

Figure 1 Two axes of subordination.

insights and, with additional brainstorming on our part, will yield more precise predictions about intergroup politics in the pages that follow. Notice that each group's position is relative to the other. In other words, it is very nearly impossible to understand, say, the position of Asian Americans without also appreciating where African Americans, Latinos, and Whites are located on this plane. This relational arrangement will become critical as we begin developing our hypotheses about *interminority* politics (cf. Turner et al. 1987).

In fact, if you look closely, you can better appreciate that most non-White groups hold a relatively more privileged rank in comparison to other groups. For example, although many REP scholars are well aware of the types of advantages that Whites enjoy relative to non-Whites, what has been less clear is how each non-White group enjoys a modicum of advantage with respect to other people of color. We say modicum because the edges they possess here are based on real, but small rays of light peeking in between groups. For example, while all non-White groups are marginalized, Blacks are stereotyped as a relatively more *American* group than other people of color. Similarly, inasmuch as Asians are stereotyped as a more *foreign* group than Black and White individuals, they are also stereotyped as relatively *superior* to their Latino and Black counterparts. Alas, these small but invidious comparisons can fuel a "narcissism of small differences," such that any advantage within this hierarchical arrangement, no matter how small or seemingly petty, will trigger the types of intergroup comparisons that often produce in-group favoritism – a behavioral bias toward one's immediate in-group (Billig and Tajfel 1973; Tajfel 1981; Tajfel et al. 1971; Tajfel and Turner 1986).

We deem these relative advantages as primarily psychological, with the added punch that they can strongly motivate individual *political* behavior. In fact, we reason that non-Whites' stances toward other communities of color depend, critically, on their own location within this system: how *inferior* do I sense my group to be (relative to others) and how *foreign* do I believe my group is (relative to others) (Zou and Cheryan 2017)? To illustrate this, consider that while African Americans are often treated as a socially *inferior* group, they are also viewed as more *American* than Asians and Latinos. In contrast, although Asians are viewed as more *foreign* than other groups, they are also viewed as more *superior* than Blacks and Latinos.

To further distinguish our model from alternatives, we call attention to the motivations it highlights among people of color. Our model, like others, stresses notions of group status (e.g., Gusfield 1963; Hoffstadter 1965; Mutz 2018; Parker and Barreto 2013), which are often steeped in *symbolic* conflicts over "conflicting ways of life" (Blum and Parker 2019: 739). Perhaps the most well-known example here is White individuals' strong sense of ownership over the United States, its culture, it customs, and its traditional ways of life (Danbold and Huo 2015; Pérez et al. 2019). Indeed, as Devos and Banaji (2005) demonstrated a while back, for many White individuals, to be American *is* to be White (and vice versa). Thus, when this status undermined – say, by the growing number of people of color (Craig and Richeson 2014; Danbold and Huo 2015; Pérez 2021) – they will lash out politically by expressing attitudes and behaviors that help them repair this sense of loss. In our framework, status threats also arise among people of color, but their source is different. In particular, communities of color are sensitive to their relatively unique position in the racial order as a more socially *superior* minority group (e.g., Asian individuals) or a more *American* community of color (e.g., Black individuals). This contrasts sharply with group-conflict models, such as realistic group conflict theory (Sherif et al. 1961), where threats emanate from competition over a finite resource, such as jobs or housing.

Our reasoning, then, draws on three major assumptions. First, all individuals recognize this more intricate racial order. Second, members of each racial group acknowledge their own position, and the position of others, within this hierarchy, with each position bound up with particular "ways of life" that are "owned" by some groups (Waldzus et al. 2004; Wenzel, Mummendey, and

Waldzus 2007). Third, and perhaps most importantly, each category within the hierarchy is actually comprised of a mega-group that finds coherence and meaning via its implied comparisons with other out-groups in the racial order (cf. Gaertner et al. 1999; Mason 2018; Transue 2007). Thus, Mexicans, Puerto Ricans, Cubans, and other national-origin groups operate as *Latino* in comparison to non-Latino groups (Beltrán 2010). Similarly, Chinese, Filipinos, Koreans, and other national-origin groups operate as *Asian* in comparison to non-Asian groups (Tuan 1998). These nuances are important and become critical when studying *intra*group dynamics. Yet our focus here is on *inter*group dynamics, which means that within-group differences recede while between-group differences come to the fore (cf. Turner et al. 1987).[1]

But can we really take these three points for granted and then move forward to distill new predictions about political behavior? Although Zou and Cheryan (2017) present some evidence of these assumptions, we extend their work here by using richer and more contemporary survey data to further validate them (see also Craig et al. n.d.).

The data we employ are based on the 2020 Pilot American National Election Study (ANES): a comprehensive online survey of (non-)White adults containing extensive measures of people's stereotypes about other groups as *superior* and *American*. In particular, White ($n = 1,140$), Black ($n = 219$), Latino ($n = 193$) and Asian ($n = 76$) adults were asked to use a scale from 1 to 7 to rate how *intelligent (versus unintelligent)* they believe each of these racial groups is. Following Zou and Cheryan's (2017) lead, we treat this item as a crisp indicator of a group's perceived *superiority*. In addition, respondents also completed ratings of Whites, Blacks, Latinos, and Asians as *American* versus *foreign*, and *patriotic* versus *unpatriotic*, each time using this same 1-to-7 scale. We recode these responses so that higher values indicate stronger belief that a group is *American*. Given their high degree of intercorrelation across respondents ($\alpha = 0.859$), we average them for each racial group under analysis. For both measures, higher values reflect greater belief that a specific racial group is more *superior* or more *American*.

Figure 2 displays these values. There we can appreciate the general patterns that are implied by our discussion of the two axes of subordination within

---

[1] It bears mentioning that Black Americans and (non-Hispanic) Whites are also mega-groups in the sense that they, too, encompass a variety of national origins and experiences, although they are not typically construed as such. Consider that "Black" encapsulates a variety of national origins, including those with roots in contemporary sub-Saharan Africa and the Caribbean (Greer 2013; Rogers 2006; Watts Smith 2014). Similarly, "White" consists of a variety of European and non-European groups (Ignatiev 1995; Jacobson 1998). These internal shades of difference are important to recognize and can lead to *intra*group tension when one group (e.g., Mexicans) is highlighted as an out-group for others (e.g., Cubans). But in our analysis, the out-group is "out there," in another part of the hierarchy, which serves to minimize the perceived heterogeneity of one's larger in-group (i.e., Latinos, Blacks, Asians, Whites).

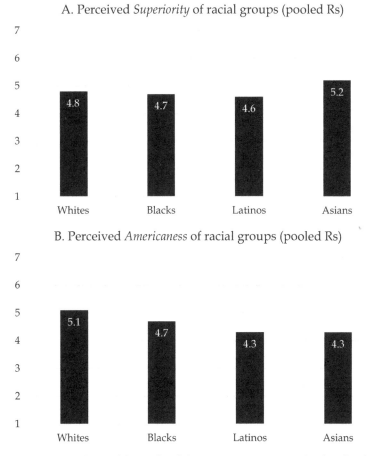

Figure 2 Pooled rankings of racial groups on two axes of subordination.

America's racial order. Consider panel A, which depicts pooled ratings of all four racial and ethnic groups along the *superiority* dimension. Consistent with expectations, one sees that African Americans and Latinos are deemed to be less *superior* than are Whites. Also in line with our reasoning, Asian Americans are considered to be more *superior* than both African Americans and Latinos. All of these differences are significant at the 5 percent level or better via paired *t*-tests. The one wrinkle in these patterns is that Asian Americans are rated as significantly more *superior* than Whites. This discrepancy could be due to our use of perceived *intelligence* as our sole operationalization of *superiority* in this context. Indeed, emerging research suggests that in some contexts, White and Asian individuals perceive the latter to be more academically inclined than the former (Jiménez 2017; Jiménez and Horowitz 2013).

And what about people's perceptions of how *American* these same groups are? Panel B in Figure 2 reveals even sharper evidence of this dimension's meaningfulness. In particular, we find, consistent with our reasoning, that Whites are perceived as *the* most *American* group. In further adherence to our claims, we also observe that Blacks are considered significantly more *American* than are Latinos and Asians, both of whom are rated as significantly less *American* than are Whites and Blacks. All of these differences, again, are significant at the 5 percent level or better via paired *t*-tests.

In raw form, the ratings just presented give us an intuitive look at how the two axes of subordination operate. But missing from these depictions is an even crisper sense of their relativity, both in terms of how each non-White group compares to Whites – the dominant group in the hierarchy – as well as how members of each racial group construe these relative comparisons. To clarify the picture here, we first take our *superiority* ratings for each non-White group and subtract individuals' ratings of Whites on this dimension. Given that the RPM's insight about each subordinate group is with respect to the dominant group (i.e., Whites), we believe these differenced measures yield additional conceptual light. Thus, for each subordinate group in question, we produce a measure that captures individuals' sense of how *superior* one believes a subordinate group is relative to Whites: the most privileged category on both axes of America's racial order. This means that positive values on these differenced measures indicate a subordinate group is deemed more *superior* in comparison to Whites, while negative values indicate a subordinate group that is deemed more *inferior* with respect to Whites. Figure 3 displays these relative rankings for the *superiority* dimension.

Per the RPM, we anticipate variability in these *superiority* ratings, with individuals considering some groups as having higher status than others. Key to all this are the comparisons *between* these relative ratings. Figure 3 indicates that White individuals in this survey believe Asian Americans are more superior than are African Americans and Latinos, since the relative rating of Asian Americans is positive for them, yet negative for Blacks and Latinos. This perceived pecking order, however, is not just a figment of White people's minds, for African Americans, Latinos, and Asians also generally display a schedule of stations that is consistent with the RPM. Notice that all non-White respondents consistently rate Asian Americans in the *superior* range of this scale, and generally higher than the other two groups of color. Indeed, respondents in this sample rank Asian Americans as a much more *superior* group than Latinos and, in most instances, a more *superior* group than African Americans. The only exception in this sample is among African American respondents, who rate their own racial group as slightly more *superior* than

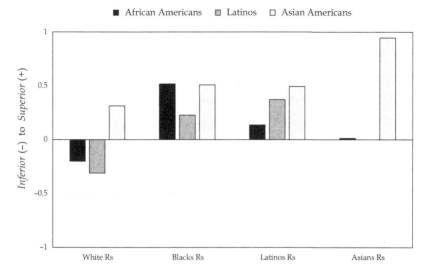

Figure 3 Perceived *superiority* of groups relative to Whites.

Asian Americans. Although this gap is statistically unreliable, it is highly consistent with the expression of in-group favoritism (Tajfel 1981) among individuals who are regularly marginalized on the basis of their race (Branscombe, Schmitt, and Harvey 1999). That is, African American individuals seem to rate their racial group as more superior than Asian Americans (and Latinos) as a way to bolster themselves against chronic hostility toward their in-group. Nevertheless, both in the aggregate and among members of specific racial groups, individuals appear to generally perceive the relative ordering of groups on this *superiority* dimension as implied by our conceptual discussion, with Asian Americans as more *superior* in comparison to other people of color.

What happens when we turn to the other dimension of the hierarchy, which involves a group's stereotyping as *American* (vs. *foreigner*)? Using the same reasoning as before, we take each non-White group's rating as *American* and subtract one's rating of Whites on this axis, thus providing a sense of each non-White group's relative standing in terms of how *American* they are perceived to be with respect to Whites. Figure 4 displays these ratings, and we can see a pattern of results that is highly consistent with our assumptions about the relative ordering of groups on this dimension. In particular, US adults generally agree that African Americans are a more *American* group than either Latinos or Asian Americans. This trend consistently emerges across all groups of respondents. Notice that most respondents generally rate Blacks as a less foreign group than other people of color. That is, respondents in this sample generally believe that African Americans are a relatively more *American* group than are Latinos

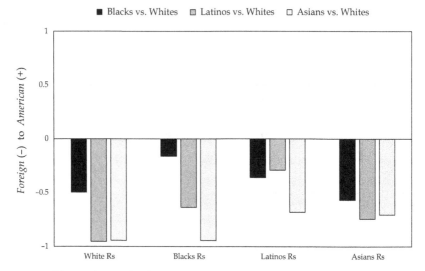

Figure 4 Perceived *Americanness* of groups relative to Whites.

and Asians – the two groups with substantial numbers of immigrants within their ranks. Indeed, although Black respondents strongly view their own group as being substantially more *American* than other people of color, it is also the case that Latinos *and* Asian Americans see Black individuals as less *foreign* than their own respective groups, as indicated by the relatively smaller negative scores they assign to Black individuals.

Taken as a whole, the evidence in Figures 2 through 4 suggests that each group is cognizant of its own placement within this cage that is America's racial order. But is there any connection between these perceptions and the politics that individuals express? We think there should be. Otherwise, what we have is evidence that groups stereotype each other on the key dimensions isolated by the RPM, but without placement within this order influencing their political outlook and behavior. To start getting a better handle on this, we return to the 2020 ANES Pilot to analyze people's opinions about undocumented immigration: a domain that strongly implicates Latinos, while raising strong concerns about how *un-American* and *inferior* unauthorized immigrants are (Pérez 2016, 2010).

The 2020 Pilot ANES fielded four items gauging support for policy measures addressing undocumented immigration, which we combine into a reliable scale ($\alpha = 0.730$). *Support border wall* queried, "Do you favor, oppose, or neither favor nor oppose building a wall on the US border with Mexico?," with 1-favor a great deal to 7-oppose a great deal. The remaining items used a scale from 1-strongly favor to 5-strongly oppose. *Oppose citizenship pathway* probed about "Providing a path to citizenship for unauthorized immigrants who obey the law, pay a fine, and pass security checks." *Maintain penalties for undocumented immigrants* explored "Ending criminal penalties for people crossing the border illegally." Finally, *Deport unauthorized immigrants* gauged "Returning all unauthorized immigrants to their native countries." All four outcomes are coded so that higher values reflect stronger immigration opposition. Thus, in our index of opposition to undocumented immigration, higher values reflect greater distaste for this type of migratory flow.

Using this scale, we examine the correlation between opposition to undocumented immigration and one's perceptions of Latinos as more *superior* and *American*, net of other individual differences, such as partisanship, education levels, age, and gender. Table 1 reports the core results, focusing on the stereotypes that people have about Latinos and their impact on opposition to unauthorized immigration. We exclude the few number of Asian respondents ($n = 76$) from this analysis, given that their low numbers make any parametric analysis here quite uninformative.

Table 1 reports a set of results that align with core insights of the RPM. Take the entries for White individuals. In the row labeled "More American," we see that a stronger sense of viewing Whites as more *American* than Latinos is positively and reliably associated with expressed opposition to undocumented immigration (0.475) among White respondents. Similarly, a stronger belief that Whites are more *superior* to Latinos is similarly correlated in a positive and reliably way with opposition to undocumented immigration (0.333) among

Table 1 Relevant axes predict White, Black, and Latino opposition to undocumented immigration

	Whites	**Blacks**	**Latinos**
More American	0.475*	0.404*	
(relative to Latinos)	(0.087)	(0.200)	
More superior	0.333*	0.085	
(relative to Latinos)	(0.097)	(0.207)	
N	1,133	216	
More American (relative to Whites)			0.143
			(0.201)
More superior (relative to Whites)			−0.296
			(0.207)
N			192

Note: All tests are two-tailed. $*p < 0.05$

White adults. These patterns align with the view that Whites are deemed the most *American* and *superior* group in the hierarchy.

Now turn to the results for Black individuals. According to the RPM, Blacks' relative positioning as a more *American* minority group should be related to how they view the issue of undocumented immigration. And it is. Holding constant the influence of Blacks' sense of *superiority*, those Black adults who believe they are more *American* than Latinos report reliably stronger opposition to unauthorized immigration (0.404). This pattern is consistent with Zou and Cheryan's work on the two axes of subordination, as well as Niambi Carter's (2019) insights about the importance of being American to Black individuals in the United States.

And what about Latinos, a group which is positioned differently than Whites and Blacks within the racial order and strongly implicated by the realm of undocumented immigration? What we observe is that Latinos' sense of being more *American* is hardly associated with their opinions about unauthorized immigration. This is unsurprising given that the issue of "illegal" immigration makes salient notions of being *American* – a plane along which Latinos are strongly marginalized (Pérez 2016). Yet we do see that on the other dimension, Latinos' sense of *superiority* is more meaningfully associated with their views of unauthorized immigration. In particular, the more that Latinos see themselves as *superior*, the less opposed to undocumented immigration they are, although the effect is statistically imprecise (-0.296, $p < 0.155$, two-tailed) given the smaller number of Latinos in this sample ($n = 192$).

Taken together, these correlational results provide some provisional evidence about the possible linkages between one's position in the racial order and one's political response. But as tantalizing as these findings may seem, they leave behind too many loose ends, especially with respect to the mechanisms that underpin any connections between one's position in the racial hierarchy and the political response to others. Alas, it is one thing to observe a correlation between rankings in the racial order and policy views toward a minority out-group; it is quite another to show that those patterns emerge because of a sense of threat to one's more advantageous position within America's racial hierarchy. But that is precisely what our argument is: that when threatened, the more privileged location of one's group in America's racial order leads people of color to defend this beachhead – a defensive posture that can undermine any shared sense of solidarity among groups who have been "left holding the bag" in terms of inequality for quite some time (Pérez 2021). In order for us to make this inferential leap, we will need to drill down further into the political psychology that underpins the outlooks of people of color. We begin this task by first centering on the case of African Americans and their political posture toward Latinos.

3 Not More American than Me: Black Reactions to Latino Growth

In the study of race, ethnicity, and politics, African Americans are a paradigmatic case, as well as an exceptional one. They are paradigmatic insofar as they are *the* paragon for how systematic exclusion and subjugation on the count of race can produce an enduring sense of identity, one that is chronically accessible and highly influential on political attitudes and behavior (e.g., Block 2011; Brown and Davis 2002; Dawson 1994, 2000; Harris-Lacewell 2004; McClain et al. 2009; White and Laird 2020; White, Laird, and Allen 2014). Indeed, African Americans sharply illustrate how stable racial identities can inspire effective collective action in American politics (Dawson 1994; Lee 2002; White and Laird 2020). Thus, one of the pictures emerging from the study of Black politics is of a community where a sense of racial marginalization colors many of the ways in which African Americans perceive and engage with politics at various levels – an influential blueprint for how researchers study the identity-to-politics link among other non-White groups (Barreto 2007; Junn and Masuoka 2008; Kuo et al. 2017; Lajevardi 2020; Lee 2008; Lien et al. 2004; Oskooii 2020; Pérez 2015a, 2015b; Pérez et al. 2019; Sanchez and Masuoka 2010).

But African Americans are also an exceptional case because of their complicated and tense relationship with the American nation (Citrin et al. 2001; DuBois 1903; Higginbotham 1993). Knowledgeable observers of African American politics point out, correctly, that the stain of chattel slavery is what distinguishes the Black experience from the experiences of other non-Whites (Dawson 2000; Franklin 1947; Omi and Winant 1986; Sears and Savalei 2006). The forcible capture of individuals and their brutal transplanting to a new continent is *sui generis* of the Black community. Yet what escapes some analysts is that for many Black individuals, the experience of being American is nonetheless a "unique part of the black struggle for inclusion in this country" (Carter 2019: 43). Indeed, as Niambi Carter insightfully teaches us, "despite their maltreatment, . . . [Black people] claim some form of . . . American identity that they use to assert the primacy of their claims in the . . . hierarchy" (Carter 2019: 59). This aligns neatly with the insights of other scholars, like Mia Tuan (1998: 8), who explains how "Blacks may be many things" in the minds of people, "but foreign is not one of them."

One logical conclusion from this discussion is that despite being relegated to a more *inferior* corner of the racial hierarchy, Black people's sense of being *American* is crucial to how they sometimes behave politically (Carter 2019;

Carter and Pérez 2016; Parker 2009). That, at least, is our contention. More specifically, we argue that when Blacks' position as a relatively more *American* group is undermined, they will react with a defensive political posture that allows them to shore up this unsettled position. Yet in the absence of such threats to one's sense of being *American*, we predict that Black individuals will display the types of solidarity-based responses one might intuitively expect from one minority group toward another that shares a similar social station (e.g., Cortland et al. 2017; Pérez 2021; Sirin, Villalobos, and Valentino 2016).

Besides being falsifiable, the virtue of this *American edge* hypothesis is its conditional nature. It implies, first, that African Americans are a product of their unique circumstance, for they can react on the basis of experiences emanating from their alleged *inferior* status or on the basis of how *American* they are considered to be. Which of these routes is followed by Black individuals depends on whether – and when – they sense a threat to their rank as a more *American* minority group. Second, our *American edge* hypothesis implies that when Blacks' sense of being a more *American* minority group is jeopardized, it will affect not only what Black individuals believe and feel toward other people of color, but also how they behave politically toward them – again, with these reactions serving to restore Blacks' relative advantage as a more *American* minority in the racial order.

We lay our reasoning utterly bare here because we think our interpretation of Blacks' stance vis-à-vis other people of color is a far different one than those proposed by other authors (e.g., Gay 2006; McClain et al. 2007; Sniderman and Piazza 2002). For example, a simpler construal of Black intolerance toward other people of color would have us believe that Black individuals can sometimes be just as prejudiced as Whites. Yet this needlessly characterizes Black people's defensive posture toward other racial minorities as individually pathological, rather than highly adaptive and sensitive to status considerations that are *fluid* (i.e., Black individuals are not always intolerant of other minorities) (Block 2011; Brown and Davis 2002); *structural* (i.e., Black peoples' intolerance is rooted in their station within the racial hierarchy) (Zou and Cheryan 2017); and *functional* (i.e., Black people are psychologically motivated to restore their group's more advantaged position in the racial order) (Katz 1960; Tajfel and Turner 1986). The challenge, then, is differentiating our more involved interpretation of African Americans' stance toward other people of color relative to a more parsimonious alternative – a feat that requires original and more surgically precise data.

3.1 Probing the Minds of Black Individuals

Our claim is that African Americans are sometimes motivated to express intolerant attitudes and opinions toward other people of color in an effort to reassert what they sense is their more advantaged position as *Americans* in the racial order. This is a sequential, chain-linked argument, where political circumstances threaten Black individuals' sense that they are more *American* than other racial minorities, which then generates downstream impacts on their political reaction to other non-White groups. How can we validate these path-driven effects?

The answer is what, statistically, is known as mediation analysis (Baron and Kenny 1986; Danbold and Huo 2015; Pérez et al. 2019; Zhao, Lynch, and Chen 2010). The intuition behind this approach is that the effect of an underlying cause is transmitted to an outcome *indirectly* through an intervening variable, which often captures some motivation. In the case at hand, our *American edge* hypothesis implies that a threat to Black people's unique position in the racial order will unsettle their sense of being a more *American* minority group. This jeopardized status should then yield downstream consequences for Black individuals' political views and judgments of other people of color, especially those groups deemed responsible for Black peoples' sense of lost status. The motivation driving Black individuals' response in this circumstance is a need to recapture what they feel is their relative position as a more *American* minority group.

3.2 An Experiment on Black-Latino Relations

We test this proposed mechanism in the realm of Black-Latino relations, which has produced reams of research into determining whether these are characterized more by conflict or cooperation (cf. Benjamin 2017; Cutaia Wilkinson 2015; McClain and Karnig 1990; McClain et al. 2005). In our rendition of things, the presence of conflictual or cooperative relations between these groups is a matter of social circumstance – as captured by America's racial hierarchy – rather than innately driven by each group's feelings and prejudices toward others.

In the case of Black-Latino relations, African Americans are positioned as a relatively more *American* minority group than Latinos. Hence, our reasoning implies that a threat to Black people's edge as a more *American* group should influence their political and social response to Latinos, the out-group in focus here. To evaluate this proposition, we designed the "Unsettled American" Experiment, which we undertook via Prolific, an online participant panel for academic research.

Specifically, we collected a sample of US-born Black adults ($n = 409$), which we randomly allocated across four conditions.[2] In each condition, Black

---

[2] Given that *African American* is a racial category, while *Latino* is an ethnic one, it is possible that a few individuals in this sample are Afro-Latino (e.g., Puerto Ricans who self-classify themselves as Black in racial terms). However, for the purpose of our framework and experiment, what is critical is whether multifaceted individuals, like Afro-Latinos, recognize and are invested in the unique position of African Americans in the US racial order, especially with respect to an out-

participants read information about (1) geographic mobility (*control*); (2) Latino demographic growth changing US culture (*American status threat*); (3) Latino growth dragging down the quality of immigrants (*Immigrant status threat*); or (4) Latino growth increasing interminority competition in politics (*realistic threat*). This last condition directly acknowledges the role that competition over material resources – in this case, political seats – can sometimes play in triggering interminority conflict, as established by prior work (cf. Benjamin 2017; Cutaia Wilkinson 2015; McClain and Karnig 1990; Sniderman and Piazza 2002). Hence, in order for our argument to hold water empirically, the sense of threat that Black adults feel from a jeopardized sense of being *American* must be independent of any sense of material threat they feel from another group, like Latinos.[3]

In the interest of space, we report the full details of these various conditions in Appendix A.1. But to provide readers with a firm grasp of our manipulations, Figure 5 displays the visuals and language used in our *American threat* condition, the focal treatment in this study. Careful perusal of this treatment should convey a few things. First, notice the visuals here relay that Latinos are growing demographically at a clipping pace, which is consistent with actual trends as reported by the US Census Bureau and media outlets (cf. Craig and Richeson 2014). In fact, the first plot and language attending it are a direct adaptation of an effective manipulation designed by Craig and Richeson (2018). Second, the visuals also display an alleged consequence of this growth, namely, the presence of individuals with weaker fluency in America's language, English. Both of these visuals affirm the major points that are detailed in the treatment's text, which underlines the heightened growth of Latinos vis-à-vis other minority groups (including Black individuals) and the implications of this growth for the definition of *Americans*. In order to stress this latter point, this treatment also showcases a putatively Black person, *Tyrone Washington*, who laments how an increase in Latinos is complicating the definition of what it means to be *American*. What still remains to be seen is whether, in light of ingesting this message, Black Americans react in the way we expect they will.

---

group. The evidence for this is whether our proposed experiment "works" by triggering the anticipated reaction among self-identified Black adults (irrespective of whether they are ethnically Latino or not).

[3] Since we wish to compare the reactions of African Americans to Asian Americans, we manipulated *realistic threat* by focusing on its political dimension. Although some research suggests that Black Americans and Latino immigrants compete for jobs in similar economic niches (Carter 2019; Diamond 1998), Asian Americans and Latinos generally inhabit distinct labor markets, with a large presence of Asian immigrants in high-tech industries (Junn 2007; Malhotra, Margalit, and Mo 2013). This nuance is unlikely to make a realistic economic threat resonate with Asian participants. However, we reasoned that a realistic political threat would be more credible with both Black *and* Asian American participants.

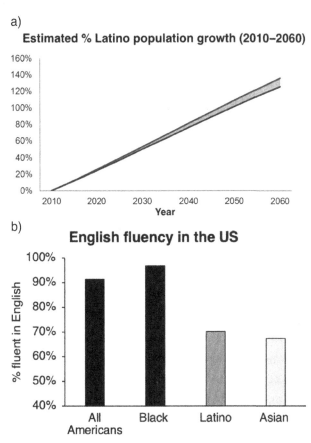

Figure 5 Treatment: *American threat* condition.
Participants were presented with the shown figures and text.

New U.S. Census Bureau data reveal that Latinos are a rapidly growing ethnic group, making it the largest of the three major ethnic minority populations in the United States (i.e., Asians, Latinos, and Blacks). According to Census Bureau data, the Latino population is expected to more than double in the next forty years, increasing four times faster than the total US population. A greater Latino presence in communities throughout the country is redefining what it means to be an American in major ways.

Indeed, in a community with a substantial Latino population, long-time resident Tyrone Washington said, "I used to think that being American was about speaking English, eating cheeseburgers, and following American politics. But when I see Latinos, I see people who live here in the United States, yet want to speak Spanish, eat pozole and mondongo, and follow their home country's politics. Unlike the rest of us, Latinos don't seem to be a part of the American way of life and are instead trying to transform the U.S. into their own culture and image."

3.3 Mediators: Black Americans' Sense of Position Along Two Axes

Following assignment to one of these experimental conditions, Black participants completed several items appraising our mediators, that is, people's perceptions of each dimension in the racial order. By design, then, we treat a sense of threat as exogenous (which we manipulate experimentally), while perceptions of the racial order are endogenous. This latter part of our specification is facilitated by the fact that these perceptions are correlated with, but conceptually distinct from, a person's sense of racial and national identity (Zou and Cheryan 2017). Hence, they should become unsettled in light of threat.[4]

For readers who might worry that this design omits or ignores the well-established influence of racial identity on Black people's orientation toward public affairs (Dawson 1994; White 2007; White, Laird, and Allen 2014), we call attention to how each dimension in the racial order aligns with Black individuals' sense of racial and national identity. As W. E. B. Dubois (1903) and others (Citrin et al. 2001) have observed, Black individuals often experience a sense of "double consciousness," such that their racial and national identities are in tension with each other. This complexity is captured by the two dimensions of the racial order. The *foreign-American* axis reflects the plane on which African Americans are relatively more distinct than other people of color. In turn, the *inferior-superior* axis indicates the corridor that Black individuals share with other people of color, where they are marginalized on the basis of a variety of ascriptive racial and ethnic characteristics (e.g., skin tone, language, etc.).

Accordingly, the first of our mediators taps into perceptions of the category *American*, which sits along the *foreigner-American* axis where African Americans are stereotyped as more *American* than other non-Whites. The second mediator involves perceptions of the category *Immigrant*, which is designed to reflect the *inferiority-superiority* axis in the racial order. This is the dimension along which Asian Americans are stereotyped as a higher-status group than other people of color. Since Asians' higher level of prestige is sustained by heavy flows of high-skill immigration from Asian countries (Junn 2007; Zou and Cheryan 2017), we operationalize this axis via the category *Immigrant*. By appraising perceptions of these two categories, *American* and *Immigrant*, we position ourselves to observe whether Black

---

[4] This same reasoning also shapes our design of a parallel experiment with Asian American adults, which we analyze in the next chapter.

people's reaction (and later in the monograph, Asian people's reaction) to another community of color is truly motivated, as we say, by their relative advantage within the racial order – in this case, Black individuals' rank as a community of color that is stereotyped as more *American*.[5]

To this end, Black participants were asked "To what extent is the following important for being truly American?" with three attributes rated on scales from 1-not at all important to 7-extermely important: (1) Having been born in America; (2) Having lived in America for most of one's life; and (3) Having American citizenship (Jardina 2019). Participants were also asked "To what extent are the following qualities important to being an immigrant in the United States?," with three attributes evaluated on the same scale: (1) Having specialized or technical skills; (2) Possessing high levels of education; and (3) Entering the country legally and following established procedures. The order of these two batteries was randomized.

3.4 Outcomes: Social and Political Reactions to Latinos

Following the assessment of our mediators, Black participants completed a broad suite of outcomes: (1) *favorability toward people of color*; (2) *support for English-only policy*; (3) *opposition to immigration*; and (4) *pro-environment preferences*, which we administer as a placebo to gauge how racialized Black respondents' political reactions are in light of threat to their ranking in the racial order.

We assessed *favorability toward racial and ethnic minorities* with an item asking participants to use a scale from 1-unfavorable to 7-favorable to indicate "How do you feel toward … ?," with the relevant groups being Asians, Blacks, Latinos, and Whites. We transform these ratings into differenced measures, where we take one's expressed feelings toward a specific minority group and subtract from it one's rating of Whites, thus leaving us with three different indicators of favorability toward people of color.

We also tapped opinions toward political groups and policies, with most of the latter strongly implicating Latinos. Specifically, we assessed *support for English-only policy* with a single statement, "Establish English as the official US language," which was completed on a scale from 1-strongly oppose to 7-strongly support. Using this same scale, participants completed four other

---

[5] Later in the manuscript, we will repeat this same study to observe whether Asian Americans, in contrast to African Americans, respond to another community of color on the basis of their relative advantage as a higher-status group whose prestige is strongly tied to high-skill immigration from Asia.

statements gauging *opposition to immigration:* "Increase the time required for immigrations to become eligible for US citizenship," "Decrease the level of federal resources for arresting undocumented immigrants," "Renew temporary relief from deportation for young undocumented immigrants," and "Provide a pathway to citizenship for undocumented immigrants."

Finally, to assess our placebo, *pro-environment preferences*, participants answered three items on the same 7-point scale as before: "Levy a green tax on gasoline to help protect the environment," "Give the Environmental Protection Agency (EPA) the authority to regulate carbon dioxide emissions," and "Raise the required fuel efficiency for the average automobile from 25 mpg to 35 mpg to reduce environmental pollution."

3.5 Black Reactions to Latinos Are Driven by a Perceived Loss of American Status

Our reasoning suggests that threats to the more privileged rank of a minority group in the racial order should generate a defensive reaction toward other minority out-groups. Key to this hypothesis are shifts in Black views of the category *American*, but not the category *Immigrant*, since we contend that Black individuals' relative advantage in the racial order is rooted in their sense of being more *American*. Since we measured Black perceptions of *American* and *Immigrant* with three items each, we validate them through a confirmatory factor analysis (CFA).

We find that four out of these six items capture their intended construct well, leaving us with two items to measure *American perceptions* ($\alpha = 0.81$) and two items to gauge *Immigrant perceptions* ($\alpha = 0.87$). The weaker-performing items are *Having American citizenship* and *Entering the country legally and following established procedures*, which tap their respective construct, yet still remain robustly correlated with each other ($r = 0.400$, $p < 0.01$, two-tailed). This suggests these latter items fail to crisply distinguish between both mediators, so we drop them from further analyses.

Table 2 reports a revised CFA with just four items and it displays excellent fit.[6] Since our CFA was estimated with all items in their native metric, the coefficients here represent shifts of nearly 1 point. Thus, a 1-point

---

[6] In the initial six-item model, the CFA's overall fit was incredibly poor, with a CFI/TLI below their recommended 0.90 thresholds, and an RMSEA surpassing its advised 0.08 level. The improved fit of Table 2's CFA is not a function of lower degrees of freedom. Indeed, if we "buy" ourselves some wiggle room by constraining to equality the item loadings for each mediator, the fit of this second, better-fitting CFA still does not budge, while the loadings remain substantively and statistically significant (Brown 2007).

Table 2 Confirmatory factor analyses of mediator items (African Americans)

Items		
Important to be US-born	1.720*	
	(0.121)	
Important to live in USA for a long time	1.642*	
	(0.115)	
Important to have US citizenship	–	
Important to have technical skills		1.654*
		(0.104)
Important to have higher education		1.793*
		(0.104)
Important to immigrant legally		–
Inter-factor correlation	0.472*	
CFI/TLI	1.000/1.000	
RMSEA [90% CI]	0.000 [0.000, 0.107]	

Note: Model estimated via full information maximum likelihood (ML) in Mplus. All variables have a 1 to 7-point metric. $N = 409$ for both models. *$p < 0.05$, two-tailed.

increase in perceptions of *American* strengthens agreement with the items "born in the US" by nearly two points (1.720). Similarly, a 1-point increase in perceptions of *Immigrant* generates a rise in agreement of nearly two points on the observed items "have technical skills" (1.654). This evidence distills into a simple, but important conclusion: this quartet of items reliably captures Black individuals' perceptions of being *American* and an *Immigrant*.

With appraisal of our mediators complete, the next step is to assess whether Latino threat to Blacks' station as a more *American* minority actually drives African Americans to express more exclusionary opinions. Given the availability of multiple items for both our mediators and many of our outcomes, we estimate a structural equation model (SEM), which allows us to: (1) attenuate measurement error in our estimates; and (2) simultaneously evaluate two possible mediators – in this case, mediators reflecting Black peoples' sense of position on both axes of America's racial order (Bollen 1989; Pérez et al. 2019; Tavits and Pérez 2019).[7]

Our SEM yields several illuminating results. First, consistent with prior work (Benjamin 2017; Cutaia Wilkinson 2015; McClain and Karnig 1990), we find that heightening a sense of *realistic threat* (relative to the control) reliably

---

[7] We report our full SEM results in the Appendix (A.2).

unsettles Black individuals' sense of being *American* (–0.338, $p < 0.030$, two-tailed). This means that any effect from our proposed trigger – threat to *American status* – must be sizeable, reliable, and additive. And it is. Relative to the control, alleging that Latino demographic growth redefines what it means to be *American* weakens Black perceptions of this category by nearly half a point (–0.482, $p < 0.002$), which is a sizeable and highly significant effect. In other words, reading about the demographic increase of Latinos leads African Americans to revise downward their perceptions of *Americans* as a category where US-born individuals or long-time US residents no longer predominate.

We construe this negative shift as an indication of perceived threat. In fact, Pérez et al. (2019) establish that revised perceptions like these are deemed threatening because the composition of *Americans* becomes more heterogeneous, which leads some individuals to favor policies that reinforce the relative coherence of this category. Finally, and in line with our theoretical reasoning, the suggestion that Latino growth is unsettling what it means to be an *Immigrant* (relative to the control) fails to impact Black Americans' sense of this category in a reliable way (0.241, $p < 0.175$, two-tailed), thus further indicating that it is Black individuals' agitated sense of being *American* that makes them feel profoundly threatened.

Consistent with this interpretation, Black Americans bounce back from their sense of threat by reporting *less* favorability toward minorities (–0.195, $p < 0.005$, two-tailed). That is, Black individuals appear to restore their sense of being *American* by expressing cooler feelings toward other people of color, which includes both Latinos and non-Latino groups. This more critical stance toward other non-Whites further manifests in the types of policies that Black Americans are willing to support. More specifically, in light of sensed threat to their position as a more *American* minority group, Black individuals report stronger support for English-only policy (0.970, $p < 0.001$, two-tailed) and more robust support for anti-immigration measures (0.413, $p < 0.001$, two-tailed). Indeed, only in the case of pro-environmental opinions – our placebo outcome – do we fail to observe this pattern (–0.090, $p < 0.230$, two-tailed). This last result is key, for it suggests that the defensive reaction manifested by Black Americans is localized and specific to intergroup issues and initiatives. That is, Black individuals react to Latino threat by expressing less generous attitudes toward Latinos and other people of color; not by displaying more miserly political attitudes in general.

These indirect effects are displayed in Figure 6, where it is easier to appreciate how Latino threat unsettles Black individuals' sense of being *American* (independently of *realistic threat*). There, one can easily trace the effect from

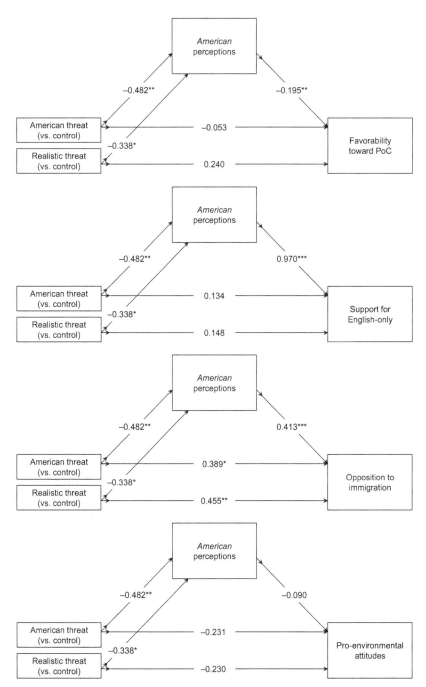

Figure 6 Unsettled views of *Americans* motivate Black political opinions.

Latinos' putative threat to being *American*, which upsets Blacks' notion of what it means to be *American*. This effect then has the downstream impact of producing more exclusionary opinions toward (non-)Latino minorities among Black individuals. In particular, Black individuals' unsettled views of the category *American* drive them to express less favorability toward people of color, more support for English-only policies, and stronger opposition to immigration. Again, only in the case of Black attitudes toward the environment (our placebo) do we fail to observe this motivated political reaction.

Table 3 further affirms our interpretation of these results by formally testing whether the indirect path from treatment(s) to each outcome via our *American* mediator is reliably different from zero (Fritz and MacKinnon 2007; Shrout and Bolger 2002). This involves evaluating whether the *joint effect* between path 1 (treatment to mediator) and path 2 (mediator to outcome) is statistically significant. Table 3 shows that when the relevant treatment is *American threat*, all of these indirect paths yield 99 percent confidence intervals that exclude zero, with the exception of our placebo (*pro-environment preferences*). This means that on all outcomes related to Latinos (e.g., *opposition to immigration*) and other people of color (e.g., *favorability toward racial and ethnic minorities*), the indirect effects from *American threat* to perceptions of *American* to our political outcomes are crisply distinguishable from zero at this level of statistical significance.

In contrast, although we find that exposure to *realistic threat* reliably unsettles Black perceptions of the category *American*, the indirect impacts of this effect on our political outcomes are not reliable at this high level of significance, since our 99 percent confidence intervals straddle zero for all outcomes under analysis. This further bolsters faith in our claim that Black individuals' negative reaction toward Latinos and other people of color emerges more reliably when they feel their own position as *Americans* is jeopardized (and independently of any sense of *realistic threat* from Latinos).

3.6 Discussion, Limitations, and Extensions

The "Unsettled American" Experiment provides consistent evidence that threats to the specific station of African Americans as a more *American* minority can motivate them to restore their jeopardized status by expressing negative political and social attitudes toward the minority out-group held responsible for that threat. In fact, we find that this reaction spills over onto other non-White groups. Thus, under more tightly controlled conditions, we observe that a threat to Black individuals' edge as a more *American* group leads them to express less unity and solidarity with Latinos and other people of

Table 3 Bootstrap tests of indirect effects (African Americans)

		Indirect effect [99% CI]
American threat > American >	Favorability toward PoC	0.094 [0.005, 0.265]
	Support English-only	−0.467 [−0.898, −0.086]
	Opposition to immigration	−0.199 [−0.435, −0.032]
	Pro-environmental opinion	0.043 [−0.051, 0.194]
Realistic threat > American >	Favorability toward PoC	0.066 [−0.007, 0.222]
	Support English-only	−0.328 [−0.765, 0.042]
	Opposition to immigration	−0.140 [−0.338, 0.021]
	Pro-environmental opinion	0.030 [−0.039, 0.160]

color, as well as stronger support for measures that curb the presence of Latinos in political life. These findings imply that Latino growth can unsettle Blacks' sense of being *American*, which motivates African Americans to push back against this threat by expressing more negative attitudes toward racial minorities *in general*.

These patterns align neatly with our *American edge* hypothesis. But at least two further objections can be raised about our inferences regarding these mediated effects. The first objection concerns our treatments. Our focal treatments include US Census data that is coupled with commentary about that information from an in-group member. Thus, for example, African Americans in all our treatment conditions read about census data documenting the high growth of the Latino population and what this means for being American, a respectable immigrant, or for Black political representation. In each instance, this data is followed by commentary by *Tyrone Washington*, a hypothetical Black individual who laments how Latinos undermine the domain in question (e.g., *American*).

We included this commentary from an in-group source so that our treatment(s) could resonate with Black participants. However, it is plausible that this source cue contaminates our treatments through social-desirability bias. That is, the negative effect we observe from *American threat* on perceptions of being *American* is not reflective of threat, as we claim, but by pressure to not appear "intolerant" or "chauvinist." In order to clarify this murkiness, we undertook Study 3, which reassesses the specific link between *American threat* and perceptions of being *American*. We do this by administering the same treatments as in Study 2, but *without* a source cue. Our faith in the conclusions we draw about Black individuals' sense of being American will be strengthened if we can show that, even in lieu of a source cue, our *American threat* treatment still unsettles Black individuals' notions of what it means to be a member of this nation by reducing their agreement with what makes one *American*.

A second objection to our inferences based on Study 2 involves the measurement of Black perceptions of being *American*, our focal mediator. Given that some of our items performed suboptimally in Study 2, our claim can benefit from additional evidence that such perceptions can be more broadly and reliably measured, per the tenets of our theory. What we require, then, is evidence that other items can also tap into Black individuals' sense of what it means to be American.

3.7 A Lab Experiment and Meta-Analysis

We address both of these concerns with a smaller lab study we conducted in winter 2019 with Black undergraduates who were part of the participant pool administered by the Race, Ethnicity, Politics & Society (REPS) Lab at UCLA, which is directed by one of the authors (Pérez). Similar to the challenges encountered by other researchers who study the psychology of non-Whites in lab settings (cf. Cortland et al. 2017; Craig and Richeson 2018), we faced real constraints in recruiting participants from a hard-to-reach population like African Americans. But with Study 2's results at our backs, plus prior published work (Zou and Cheryan 2017) on this topic, we can stipulate stronger directional hypotheses, which we can test despite a substantially smaller sample.

To this end, Study 3 recruited $n = 24$ Black participants through the REPS Lab and invited them to complete a short module on "current events in the United States." This module consisted of the same treatment arms we administered in Study 2, except *without* any source cues. Post treatment, we then administered three items gauging participants' construal of being an *American*, with the third item being entirely new. These items were statements, answered on 7-point scales, about the importance of three traits to being *American*: (1) Having been born in the US; (2) Having lived in the US for most of one's life; and (3)

Celebrating American holidays. Even with the addition of this new third item, all three statements form a reliable scale ($\alpha = 0.784$), which we score so that higher values indicate greater belief that these attributes make one American. With a measure of *American* perceptions in hand, the question is: does exposure to *American threat* once again unsettle Black individuals' sense of this category – even without a source cue? Table 4 reports the punchlines of this lab study.

In the first column, we regress Black perceptions of being *American* on each of our treatment conditions, including the one centered on *American threat*. We find that relative to the control, information alleging that Latinos undermine what it means to be a respectable *Immigrant* does not reliably impact perceptions about being *American* (-0.100, $p < 0.275$, one-tailed). Neither does exposure to the *realistic threat* that Latinos pose in politics (0.063, $p < 0.344$, one-tailed). Only in the case of exposure to threat to one's sense of being *American* do we find a sizeable effect and in the expected direction, which teeters on the border of marginal statistical significance (-0.188, $p < 0.116$, one-tailed).

Given the lack of substantive and statistical significance for the first two treatments, we collapse these conditions into an omnibus control group and reestimate the effect of *American threat*. This is the second model in Table 3. With the increase in statistical power that comes from considering just two conditions, the estimated treatment effect for *American threat* still retains its size, but is now statistically reliable at a more stringent threshold (-0.184, $p < 0.05$, one-tailed). This strengthens our conclusion that, across both studies,

Table 4 Re-assessing American threat's impact on Black individuals' perceptions of being American (Study 3, Lab)

	Being American (1)	**Being American (2)**
American threat	−0.187	−0.184*
	(0.152)	(0.106)
Immigrant threat	−0.100	–
	(0.167)	
Realistic threat	0.063	–
	(0.156)	
Constant	0.444*	–
	(0.124)	

Note: Entries are OLS coefficients with standard errors in parentheses. For each model, $n = 24$. *$p < 0.05$, one-tailed.

Black Americans' unsettled sense of being *American* is stirred by reading about the implications of Latino growth, irrespective of whether these implications are delivered (or not) by a member of one's own racial groups: this finding is robust to how we measure perceptions of the category *American*.

In fact, in order to inspire greater confidence in this inference, we meta-analyze this treatment effect on perceptions of *American* across both of our studies with Black participants (Goh et al. 2016; see also Craig and Richeson 2018; Hopkins et al. 2020). In plainer terms, a meta-analysis allows researchers to appraise whether an estimated treatment effect, across conceptually similar studies, is reliably different from zero, independent of each study's unique features. By taking this approach here, we find that our focal treatment – *American threat* – substantially and significantly upsets Black adults' perceptions about what it means to be *American*. Indeed, across these studies, *American threat* reliably threatens Black individuals' sense of being *American* by nearly one-half of a standard deviation ($d = -0.454$, s.e. $= 0.132$, $p < 0.001$, two-tailed), which is a hearty and highly reliable effect. This suggests the threat that Black individuals feel about their sense of being *American* is not dependent on whether a peer from one's racial in-group communicates this threat (or not). Our principal conclusion, then, is that Black Americans' political reactions to other people of color are strongly motivated by their unique position in America's complex racial order.

The question now, however, is whether this hierarchy also shapes the politics that other groups display toward non-Whites? We speak to this blind spot directly by turning next to the case of Asian Americans.

4 Robbing Us of Our Shine: Asian American Reactions to Latino Growth

If, in the study of race, ethnicity, and politics, African Americans are a paradigmatic but exceptional case, as we described them earlier, then Asian Americans are a seemingly unparalleled group. Asian Americans have experienced, and continue to bear the brunt of, various forms of racial discrimination (Kim 2003; King 2000; Masuoka and Junn 2013; Ngai 2004; Reny and Barreto 2020; Takaki 1989). Yet they are seemingly unparalleled in being marginalized without the type of durable and collective sense of racial identity that generally characterizes African Americans and their political attitudes and behavior (e.g., Cain, Kiewet, and Uhlaner 1991; Hajnal and Lee 2012; Junn and Masuoka 2008; Lien, Conway, and Wong 2004; Nakanishi 1991; Tam Cho 1995; Wong 2005; Wong et al. 2011). Indeed, the Asian American case stresses how the presence of racial discrimination is sometimes insufficient to catalyze collective action in US politics, particularly when a group in question is highly internally diverse, as Asian Americans are (e.g., Tam Cho 1995; Wong et al. 2011). Alas, unlike the bonding experience that slavery and its legacies have been for Black racial identity, Asian Americans are comprised of individuals from various national origin groups with different trajectories, languages, and – many times – antagonistic histories toward each other (Takaki 1989). Add to this the exceedingly high levels of socioeconomic status of many Asian immigrant families and we arrive at a picture of a fully demarcated group, complete with a label and broad membership, but without the deep sense of grievance that is strong enough to consistently motivate unified political behavior (Junn and Masuoka 2008; Kuo et al. 2017).

But Asian Americans also appear to be unparalleled in another respect. Knowledgeable observers of Asian American politics will point out, correctly, that even though this group is relegated to a lower social station than Whites, just like Black and Latino individuals are, they *do not* occupy the lowest rungs of society – and certainly not the same footholds as Black and Latino people (Jiménez 2017; Jiménez and Horowitz 2013). Indeed, as Claire Jean Kim, Jane Junn, Natalie Masuoka, and other scholars teach us (Jiménez 2017; Junn and Masuoka 2008; Kim 2003; Xu and Lee 2013; Zou and Cheryan 2017), Asian Americans are often obliquely praised for being a *model minority*, with the subtext being that they are more *superior* than other people of color in terms of social prestige, yet still not fully incorporated into civic life, similar to other non-White groups. This complicated position is structurally driven, rather than personally chosen. As the political scientist Jane Junn astutely points out:

> U.S. immigration policy creates a selection bias, favoring Asian immigrants with high levels of formal education and social standing. *Model minority* may be an accurate description of a selected set of Asians who successfully immigrated to the United States, but this description cannot be ... applied in comparison to other minority groups with different trajectories of fortune.

What we seem to have, then, is the presence of an "in-between" group, one that is clearly not White, but one, also, that is not positioned as low as Blacks or Latinos in terms of social prestige. Yet this liminal status, in many ways, says more about the nature of intergroup relations in America than about Asian Americans, in particular. Indeed, as Mia Tuan (1998: 4) observes, we must "question the assumption that material success necessarily leads to social acceptance." In this regard, Claire Jean Kim (2003) taught us long ago that Asian Americans' liminal status as a *model minority* is strong verification of a racial hierarchy that supports and reinforces White supremacy. That is because insofar as Asian Americans might be relatively valorized in comparison to more *inferior* communities of color, such as African Americans and Latinos, this praise stops quite short of full inclusion in the body politic, since Asian Americans are regularly ostracized as being unable or unwilling to become full Americans, given their profound immigrant roots (Kuo et al. 2017; Masuoka and Junn 2013; Xu and Lee 2013). Viewed from this angle, then, Asian Americans' uneasy location within the US racial order appears driven by the insistence of some scholars to force this group into America's hierarchy along a corridor that runs narrowly from *inferior* to *superior* groups (Sidanius et al. 1997; Sidanius and Petrocik 2001). Yet, as our discussion should make clear by now, the case of Asian Americans screams out for another dimension along which to place America's racial and ethnic groups.

This is where the insights of Zou and Cheryan (2017) come in handy yet again. Building on the work of Kim (2003), Xu and Lee (2013), and others (Tuan 1998), this pair of psychologists stakes out a strong claim for another dimension that captures the unique experiences of a group like Asian Americans: a category that is relatively more *superior* in comparison to some communities of color, yet less fully *American* than other groups of non-Whites – with this position being generated by the highly selected immigration flows feeding the growth of Asian American demographics in the United States. Braiding together and extending these insights, we yield our *Immigrant edge* hypothesis. According to this prediction, Asian Americans, by virtue of their ties to high-skilled immigration, attain a higher level of *superiority* with respect to Blacks, Latinos, and other people of color, yet still remain positioned as much less *American* than many of these groups. Thus, Asian American politics in intergroup settings should be highly sensitive to any perceived encroachment on this relatively higher status as a respectable immigrant group.

Besides being falsifiable, a major virtue of our *Immigrant edge* hypothesis is, again, its conditional nature. It implies that Asian Americans' social position is the consequence of unique structural circumstances, namely, an immigration policy regime that facilitates high-skilled immigration from Asian countries (Junn 2007). It also suggests that Asian American politics should be highly sensitive to threats to their reputed *superiority* with respect to other communities of color, such as Latinos and African Americans. Alas, we reason that Asian Americans will be especially responsive to perceived encroachments on their *superior* social status, since this is the axis along which Asian Americans have an advantage relative to other people of color. Finally, our *Immigrant edge* hypothesis implies that when Asians sense their relatively *superior* status is jeopardized, it should affect not only what Asian individuals believe and feel toward other people of color, but also how they behave politically toward them – again, with these reactions serving to restore Asians' station as a more *superior* minority in the racial order (i.e., as a respectable *immigrant* group).

We put our reasoning here into the sharpest relief possible because we think our interpretation of Asians' stance vis-à-vis other people of color is also a far different one than those implied by other scholarship (e.g., Bonilla-Silva 2004; Tuan 1998). Consider how a simpler characterization of Asian intolerance toward other people of color would have us believe that Asian Americans can be just as prejudiced as Whites, in part because they "want to be White," and in part because they "do not appreciate the reality of being marginalized as *inferior*" in the ways that Blacks, Latinos, and Native Americans are. By this view, Asian Americans are an exception to America's otherwise fairly rigid color line (DuBois 1903; Jiménez 2017; Lee and Bean 2010).

Yet this outlook reduces Asian Americans' defensive posture toward other racial minorities to individual pathology that is spurred by Asian individuals' utter ignorance of US racial politics ("I don't see that much racial discrimination at all") (Bonilla Silva 2004) or worse, by false consciousness ("I'm not *that* kind of minority") (Jost and Liviatan 2007). Our view, in contrast, is that Asian Americans generally scour the field of race relations in the United States and formulate political stances that are fluid and (1) highly *adaptive* (i.e., Asian individuals are not always intolerant of other minorities) (Pérez 2021; Lee Merseth 2018); (2) *structural* (i.e., Asians' intolerance is rooted in their station within the racial hierarchy) (Kim 2003; Zou and Cheryan 2017); and (3) *functional* (i.e., Asians are psychologically motivated to restore their group's more advantaged position in the racial order) (Katz 1960; Tajfel and Turner 1986). The challenge, then, is to empirically distinguish our interpretation of Asian Americans' stance toward other people of color from a more parsimonious alternative – a feat that demands highly granular and nuanced data.

4.1 Probing the Minds of Asian Individuals

Our claim is that Asian Americans are sometimes motivated to express intolerant attitudes and opinions toward other people of color in an effort to reassert what they sense is their more advantaged position as a more *superior* group in the racial order. This sense of *superior* status, we reason, is anchored by stereotypes of Asian Americans as a respectable *Immigrant* group, which depict Asian individuals as "harder-working" than African Americans, and who, unlike Latinos, immigrate to the United States "the right way," meaning through legal channels reserved for high-skilled immigrants. In this rendering, then, political circumstances will sometimes threaten Asian individuals' sense that they are a more *superior* immigrant community, which then produces a more critical and divisive political reaction toward other people of color.

We will validate this psychological chain reaction in a way that parallels our efforts to study Black reactions to other communities of color. Consequently, we designed a study that allows us to appraise the indirect effect of threats to Asian American's social position on their political stances toward other people of color (Baron and Kenny 1986; Danbold and Huo 2015; Pérez et al. 2019). Recall that in a mediation framework like ours, the effect of a treatment is transmitted to an outcome *indirectly* through an intervening variable, which often captures some underlying motivation. In the case at hand, our *Immigrant edge* hypothesis implies that a threat to Asian Americans' unique position in the racial order will unsettle their sense of being a respectable immigrant group. This jeopardized status as a more *superior* community of color should then yield downstream consequences for Asian individuals' political views and judgments of other non-Whites, especially those groups deemed responsible for Asians' lost sense of *superiority*. Hence, the motivation driving Asian individuals' response in this circumstance is a need to recapture what they feel is their relative position as a *superior* immigrant group.

4.2 An Experiment in Asian-Latino Relations

We test our proposed mechanism in the realm of Asian-Latino relations, which has produced significantly less research than the higher-profile interplay between African American and Latino communities (see McClain and Johnson Carew 2017; Telles, Sawyer, and Rivera-Salgado 2011; Vaca 2004). We see this gaping crater in the literature as additional validation of our more general claim that the Asian American experience in studies of US racial politics is treated as so special and unique that it is widely considered an exception to, rather than a fundamental part of, America's complex racial hierarchy. In contrast, our framework enshrines Asian Americans in the same lattice-like configuration of relations between (non-)Whites, which allows us to illuminate how Asian Americans respond to changing dynamics in a shared field of race relations. In this more unified view, the presence of conflictual or cooperative relations between Asian Americans and Latinos can be construed, in part, as a matter of circumstance – operationalized here by America's racial hierarchy – rather than innately driven by each group's prejudices toward others.

In the case of Asian American-Latino relations, Asian individuals are positioned as a relatively more *superior* group than Latinos. Hence, our reasoning implies that a threat to Asian individuals' edge as a higher-status immigrant community should influence their political and social response to Latinos, the out-group in focus here. To evaluate this proposition, we designed the "Unsettled Immigrant" Experiment, which we undertook online via Prolific, the same platform we used for our online experiment with Black individuals. Specifically, we collected a sample of Asian American adults ($n = 405$), which we also randomly allocated across four conditions. In each of these cells, Asian participants read information about (1) geographic mobility (*control*); (2) Latino demographic growth dragging down the quality of immigrants (*Immigrant status threat*); (3) Latino growth changing American culture (*American status threat*); or (4) Latino demographics increasing interminority competition in politics (*realistic threat*).[8]

To conserve space, we report the full details of these various conditions in our Appendix (A.3). But in order to provide readers with a firmer grasp of our manipulations, Figure 7 displays the visuals and language used in our *Immigrant threat* condition, which is the focal treatment in this study. Careful inspection of this treatment conveys several points. First, notice that the visuals here suggest that Latinos are growing demographically at a rapid tempo, which, again, aligns with actual trends as reported by the US Census Bureau and media outlets (cf. Craig and Richeson 2014, 2018). Second, the visuals depict one alleged consequence of this growth: the presence of individuals who undermine the quality of immigrants to the United States; in this case, through the lower education levels that Latinos possess, on average. Both visuals affirm the major points that are detailed in the treatment's text, which underlines the heightened growth of Latinos vis-à-vis other minority groups (including Asian individuals) and the implications of this growth for the definition of *Immigrants*, which is designed to capture the *superior* status of Asian Americans in comparison to Latinos and other *inferior* groups (e.g., Black Americans). Indeed, in order to stress this latter point, this treatment also show-cases a putatively Asian person, *Eric Hong*, who laments how an increase in Latinos is complicating the definition of what it means to be a respectable *Immigrant*.[9] What still remains to be seen is whether, in the wake of ingesting this message, Asian Americans react in the way we hypothesize they will.

4.3 Mediators: Asian Americans' Sense of Position along Two Axes

Following assignment to one of these experimental conditions, Asian participants completed items capturing our mediators – perceptions of *Immigrants*

---

[8] Again, we manipulated *realistic threat* by focusing on its political dimension in order to place Black and Asian Americans on a common plane to facilitate comparison across studies.

[9] We used the surname *Hong* for the sake of breadth, since it is a plausible East Asian or Southeast Asian last name, thus encompassing a wide swath of national origins in Asia.

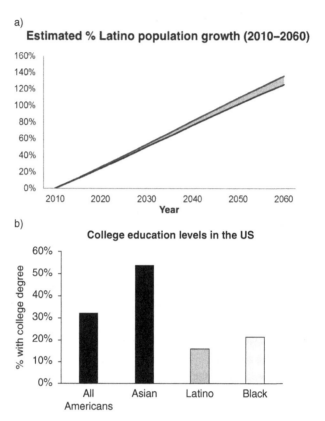

a)
Estimated % Latino population growth (2010–2060)

b)
College education levels in the US

Figure 7 Visuals and wording of *Immigrant threat* condition.
Participants were presented with the shown figures and text.

New US Census Bureau data reveal that Latinos are a rapidly growing ethnic group, making it the largest of the three major ethnic minority populations in the United States (i.e., Asians, Latinos, and Blacks). According to Census Bureau data, the Latino population is expected to more than double in the next forty years, increasing four times faster than the total US population. A greater Latino presence in communities throughout the country is redefining what it means to be an immigrant in major ways.

Indeed, in a community with a substantial Latino population, long-time resident Eric Hong said, "I used to think that being a good immigrant was about following this country's laws, providing for your own family, and sending your children to college. But when I see Latinos, I see people who break immigration laws, rely on food stamps to feed their family, and don't care about whether their children receive more than a high school education. Unlike the rest of us, Latinos are bringing down the quality of immigrants coming to and living in the United States."

and perceptions of *Americans* – which we designed to capture Asian individuals' views of the two categories that we say anchor the two axes of subordination in the US racial order. Within this hierarchy, Asian individuals are stereotyped in two distinct ways, both reaffirming their exclusion relative to Whites. On one hand, Asian Americans are generally held to be more *superior* than other people of color – a level of prestige that, we explained earlier, draws on the heavy flows of high-skill and high-education immigrants from Asian countries. On the other hand, Asian individuals are perceived to be less *American* than other non-White groups. By appraising individuals' perceptions of these two categories, *Immigrant* and *American*, we place ourselves in a position to observe whether Asian Americans' political reactions to another community of color is truly motivated, as we stipulate, by their relative advantage within the racial order – in this case, Asians' edge as a community of color that is stereotyped as more *superior* because they are a respectable group of *Immigrants*.

To this end, Asian participants were asked "To what extent are the following qualities important to being an immigrant in the United States?," with three attributes evaluated on scales from 1-not at all important to 7-extremely important: (1) Having specialized or technical skills; (2) Possessing high levels of education; and (3) Entering the country legally and following established procedures. Participants were also asked "To what extent is the following important for being truly American?," with three attributes rated on the same scales: (1) Having been born in America; (2) Having lived in America for most of one's life; and (3) Having American citizenship. The order of these two batteries was randomized across participants.

4.4 Outcomes: Social and Political Reactions to Latinos

Following the assessment of our mediators, Asian participants completed the same broad suite of outcomes that we appraised in our larger experiment with Black adults, which will allow us to closely compare our results across these studies. These outcomes were: (1) *favorability toward people of color*, (2) *support for English-only policy*, (3) *opposition to immigration*, and (4) *pro-environment preferences*, our placebo outcome.

We assessed *favorability toward racial and ethnic minorities* with an item asking participants to use a scale from 1-unfavorable to 7-favorable to indicate "How do you feel toward . . . ?," with the relevant groups being Asians, Blacks, Latinos, and Whites. We transform these ratings into differenced measures, where we again take one's expressed feelings toward a specific minority group and subtract from it one's rating of Whites, thus leaving us with three different indicators of favorability toward people of color.

In turn, we assessed *support for English-only policy* with the single statement, "Establish English as the official US language," which was completed on a scale from 1-strongly oppose to 7-strongly support. Using this same scale, participants also completed four statements gauging *opposition to immigration:* "Increase the time required for immigrations to become eligible for US citizenship," "Decrease the level of federal resources for arresting undocumented immigrants," "Renew temporary relief from deportation for young undocumented immigrants," and "Provide a pathway to citizenship for undocumented immigrants."

Finally, to assess our placebo outcome, *pro-environment preferences*, participants answered three items on the same 7-point scale as the immigration items: "Levy a green tax on gasoline to help protect the environment," "Give the Environmental Protection Agency (EPA) the authority to regulate carbon dioxide emissions," and "Raise the required fuel efficiency for the average automobile from 25 mpg to 35 mpg to reduce environmental pollution."

4.5 Asian Reactions to Latinos Are Driven by Perceived Loss of Superior Status

Our reasoning suggests that threats to the more privileged rank of a minority group in the racial order will generate a defensive reaction, manifesting in less progressive political opinions and more critical attitudes of minority outgroups. Key to this hypothesis are shifts in Asian views of the category *Immigrant*, which captures their placement along the *superior-inferior* axis of America's racial hierarchy. At the same time, however, we should not observe any meaningful shifts in Asian perceptions of the category *American*, since on that dimension, Asian individuals are at a relative disadvantage as a group that is stereotyped as being more foreign than other communities of color. Given that we originally measured Asian perceptions of *Immigrant* and *American* with three items each, we analyze them here through another confirmatory factor analysis (CFA), just as we did in our study of Black adults.

By our thinking, we expect two dimensions to underlie these six items, similar to the case of African Americans: perceptions of *Immigrant* and *American*, respectively. Thus, we model each battery of items as reflections of their corresponding category, *Immigrant* and *American*, while estimating the association between both constructs. Yet just like in our experiment with Black participants, this first model reveals a very poor fit to the data.[10] Closer inspection of the raw results suggests that, similar to the analysis of African Americans, the items *Entering the country legally and following established procedures* and *Having American citizenship* are nearly perfectly correlated with each other ($r = 0.97$, $p < 0.01$, two-tailed), strongly suggesting that these items fail to crisply distinguish between both mediators. We therefore drop these items from further analysis, leaving us with two items each to capture perceptions of *American* ($\alpha = 0.76$) and *Immigrant* ($\alpha = 0.89$).

This is reflected in the CFA reported in Table 5, which yields all signs of a well-fitting model, including item loadings that are statistically and substantively meaningful.[11] Since our CFA was estimated with all items in their native metric, these loadings reflect shifts of nearly 1 point. Specifically, a 1-point increase in perceptions of *Immigrant* yields a rise in agreement of nearly 1.5 points on the item "have technical skills" (1.427). Similarly, a 1-point increase in perceptions of *American* boosts agreement with the items "born in the US" (1.303) by comparable margins. This evidence leads us to conclude that these items reliably capture Asian individuals' perceptions of being an *Immigrant* and *American*.

With appraisal of our mediators complete, the next step is to assess whether Latinos' threat to Asians' station as a respectable *Immigrant* group actually drives Asian Americans to express more exclusionary opinions. Given the availability of multiple items for both our mediators and many of our outcomes, we again estimate a structural equation model (SEM), which allows us to: (1) attenuate measurement error in our estimates; and (2) simultaneously evaluate two possible mediators – in this case, mediators reflecting Asian individuals' sense of position on both axes of America's racial order (Bollen 1989; Pérez et al. 2019; Tavits and Pérez 2019).[12]

Our SEM generates several illuminating insights. First, we find that, unlike among African Americans, heightening a sense of *realistic threat* (relative to the control) fails to shift Asian individuals' perceptions of being an *Immigrant* (-0.051, $p < 0.731$, two-tailed) or *American* (0.084, $p < 0.609$, two-tailed). This means that for Asian Americans, their stance toward Latinos is not steeped in concerns about actual political conflict with them. What does generate

---

[10] Specifically, the CFI/TLI falls well below the recommended threshold of 0.90 and an RMSEA far above the 0.08 threshold typically recommended (Bollen 1989; Brown 2007; Pérez and Hetherington 2014).

[11] Our CFI and TLI come in at 1.00 and our RMSEA at 0.00, 90 percent CI [0.00, 0.048]. In turn, our loadings for perceptions of American and Immigrant are 1.346 and 1.471, respectively. The improved model fit is not a function of lower degrees of freedom, given our reduced number of items. If we constrain to equality each mediator's loadings, the fit of this reduced form model still does not budge (Brown 2007).

[12] We report our full SEM results in the Appendix (A.4).

Table 5 Confirmatory Factor Analyses of Mediator Items (Asian Adults)

Items		
Important to be US-born	1.303*	
	(0.113)	
Important to live in USA for a long time	1.388*	
	(0.113)	
Important to have US citizenship	–	
Important to Have technical skills		1.427*
		(0.091)
Important to have higher education		1.513*
		(0.090)
Important to immigrant legally		–
Inter-Factor Correlation	0.434*	
CFI/TLI	1.000/1.000	
RMSEA [90% CI]	0.000 [0.000, 0.100]	

Note: Model estimated via full information maximum likelihood (ML) in Mplus. All variables have a 1 to 7-point metric. $N = 405$ for both models. *$p < 0.05$, two-tailed.

a response from Asian Americans is a sense of threat to their status as a *superior* immigrant group. In comparison to the control group, alleging that Latino demographic growth is redefining what it means to be a respectable *Immigrant* weakens Asian perceptions of this category by about one quarter of a point (-0.255, $p < 0.087$, two-tailed), which is sizeable and marginally reliable. This pattern of results indicates that reading about the demographic increase of Latinos leads Asian American individuals to revise their perceptions of the category *Immigrant* downward, which Asian Americans construe as being predominated by individuals who are "high-skilled" and "follow the rules." This weakened belief in the traits reflecting *Immigrants* suggests Asian adults' views of this category were, in fact, unsettled (Pérez et al. 2019).

In contrast, neither *American threat* (0.049, $p < 0.741$) or *realistic threat* (-0.051, $p < 0.731$) measurably impacts Asian perceptions of the category *Immigrant*. Heightening the salience of Latino growth also fails to meaningfully impact Asian perceptions of the category *American* (relative to the control), which captures the other dimension in the racial hierarchy. Indeed, regardless of whether Latinos' demographic increase is framed as having implications for the definition of *Immigrants* (0.079, $p < 0.630$, two-tailed), *Americans* (0.130, $p < 0.430$, two-tailed), or for *realistic* political conflict (0.084, $p < 0.609$, two-tailed), Asian perceptions of the category *American* are substantively and statistically unaffected. This further affirms that it is Asians' agitated sense of being a respectable *Immigrant* that makes them sense a threat.

Given this pattern of results, we estimate a simpler model where we focus expressly on the sole treatment that produced a measurable impact, namely, *Immigrant status threat* and its effects on our pair of mediators. Even with the gains in statistical power that this more parsimonious model offers, *Immigrant status threat* appears to only shift Asian perceptions of *Immigrant*, with this impact now being substantively similar but more statistically precise (-0.254, $p < 0.038$, two-tailed). This suggests that exposure to *Immigrant status threat*, as we have operationalized it here, significantly unsettles Asian adults' sense of *superiority* by shifting their views about the category *Immigrant*.

In line with this interpretation, Asian Americans bounce back from this sense of threat by reporting significantly *less* favorability toward minorities (-0.189, $p < 0.004$, two-tailed). That is, Asian individuals appear to restore their sense of being a respectable *Immigrant* group by expressing cooler feelings toward people of color in general. This more critical stance toward other non-Whites further manifests in the types of policies that Asian Americans are willing to support. In the wake of a sensed threat to their relative superiority as respectable *Immigrants*, Asian individuals report reliably stronger support for English-only policy (0.344, $p < 0.001$, two-tailed) and significantly more support for anti-immigration measures (0.358, $p < 0.001$, two-tailed). Indeed, only in the case of pro-environmental opinions – our placebo outcome – do we fail to observe this pattern (-0.060, $p < 0.353$, two-tailed), which suggests that the defensive reaction manifested by Asian Americans is a reaction specific to intergroup politics. That is, Asian individuals react to Latino threat by expressing less generous attitudes toward Latinos and other people of color; not by displaying more miserly political attitudes in general.

These indirect effects are displayed in Figure 8, where it is even easier to appreciate how Latino threat unsettles Asian adults' sense of being a respectable *Immigrant*. There, one can trace the effect from the *Immigrant status threat* allegedly posed by Latinos, to being a superior *Immigrant* group – which upsets Asian notions of this category. This effect then has the downstream impact of producing more exclusionary opinions toward (non-)Latino minorities among Asian individuals.

Table 6 further affirms our interpretation of these visual results by formally testing whether the indirect path from treatment to each outcome via our *Immigrant* mediator is reliably different from zero (Fritz and MacKinnon 2007; Shrout and Bolger 2002). This involves evaluating whether the joint effect between path 1 (treatment to mediator) and path 2 (mediator to outcome) is reliably different than zero. Here, Table 6 reveals that the 95 percent

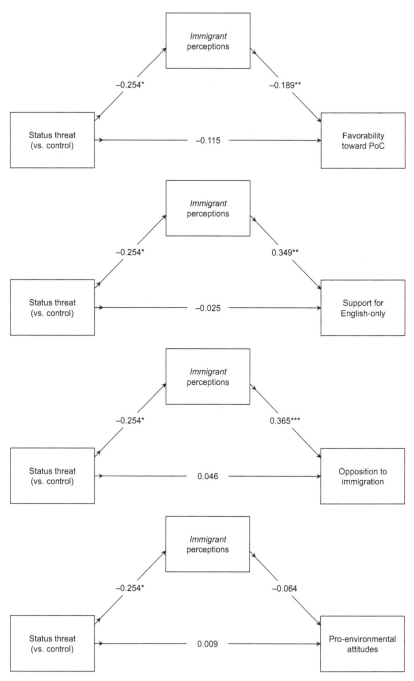

Figure 8 Unsettled views of *Immigrants* motivate Asian political opinions

Table 6 Bootstrap tests of indirect effects

		Indirect effect [95% CI]
Immigrant status threat > Immigrant >	Favorability toward PoC	0.048 [0.004, 0.124]
	Support English-only	−0.089 [−0.228, −0.009]
	Oppose immigration	−0.093 [−0.208, −0.006]
	Pro-environmental opinion	0.016 [−0.016, 0.080]

confidence intervals for these estimates generally exclude zero, with the exception of our placebo (*pro-environment preferences*). This means that on all outcomes related to Latinos (e.g., *opposition to immigration*) and other people of color (e.g., *favorability toward racial and ethnic minorities*), the indirect effect from treatment to perceptions of *Immigrant* to our political outcomes are reliably different from zero. This further shores up our claim that Asian individuals' negative reaction toward Latinos and other people of color only emerges when they feel their own position as a relatively superior *Immigrant* group is jeopardized.

4.6 Discussion, Limitations, and Extensions

The "Unsettled Immigrant" Experiment provides consistent evidence that a threat to the specific rank of Asian Americans as a more superior *Immigrant* minority can motivate them to restore their jeopardized status by expressing exclusionary political attitudes toward the minority out-group held responsible for that threat, as well as other non-White groups. Thus, under these more tightly controlled conditions, we observe that a threat to Asian individuals' edge as a superior *Immigrant* group drives them to express less unity and solidarity with Latinos and other people of color, as well as stronger support for measures that curb the presence of Latinos in political life. These findings imply that Latino growth can unsettle Asians' sense of being respectable *Immigrants*, which motivates Asian Americans to push back against this threat by expressing more negative attitudes toward racial minorities in general.

These patterns align neatly with our *Immigrant edge* hypothesis. But the same two objections that were leveled about our larger experiment with Black adults can also be raised about our inferences regarding the mediated effects we observe here among Asian American adults. If you remember, the first objection concerns our manipulations. Our focal treatments include US Census data that is coupled with commentary about that information from an in-group member. Thus, for example, Asian Americans in all our treatment conditions read about census data documenting the high growth of Latinos and what this means for being *American*, a respectable *Immigrant*, or for Asian political representation. In each instance, this data is followed by commentary by *Eric Hong*, a hypothetical Asian individual who laments how Latinos undermine the category in question (e.g., *Immigrant*).

Our justification for including this commentary from an in-group source, you may recall, was to ensure that our treatment(s) resonated with Asian participants. Yet it is plausible that this source cue contaminates our treatments through social desirability bias. That is, the negative effect we observe from *Immigrant status threat* on perceptions of being a superior *Immigrant* group are not reflective of threat, as we claim, but by pressure to not appear "chauvinistic" or "prejudiced." To dissipate this fog, we undertook another study, which reassesses this relationship between *Immigrant status threat* and perceptions of the category *Immigrant*. We do this by administering the same treatments as in our experiment with Asian adults, but *without* a source cue. Our faith in the conclusions we draw about Asian individuals' sense of being respectable *Immigrants* will be strengthened if we can show that, even in lieu of a source cue, our *Immigrant status threat* treatment still unsettles Asian adults' notions of what it means to be a member of a higher-status group by reducing their agreement with what makes one a respectable *Immigrant*.

A second objection to our inferences based on Study 4 involves the measurement of Asian perceptions of being a respectable *Immigrant* group. Given that some of our items performed suboptimally in Study 4, our claim can benefit from additional evidence that such perceptions can be more broadly and reliably measured, per the tenets of our theory. What we require, then, is evidence that other items can also tap into Asian individuals' sense of what it means to be an immigrant.

4.7 A New Lab Experiment and a Meta-Analysis

We address both of these concerns with a lab study we conducted in winter 2019 with Asian undergraduates who were part of the participant pool administered by the REPS Lab at UCLA. More specifically, Study 5 recruited $n = 142$ Asian participants through the REPS Lab and invited them to complete a short module on "current events in the United States." This module consisted of the same treatment arms we administered in Study 4, except without any source cues. Post treatment, we then administered three items gauging participants' construal of being an *Immigrant*, with the third item being entirely new. These items were statements, answered on 7-point scales, about the importance of three traits to being an *Immigrant*: (1) Having specialized or technical skills; (2) Possessing high levels of education; and (3) Having high professional ambitions. Even with the addition of this new third item, all three statements form a reliable scale ($\alpha = 0.721$), which we score so that higher values indicate greater belief that these attributes make one a respectable *Immigrant*. With a measure of these perceptions in hand, the question becomes: does exposure to *Immigrant status threat* once again unsettle Asian individuals' sense of what makes a respectable *Immigrant* – even without a source cue?

Table 7 reports the highlights of this lab study. When we regress Asian perceptions of being an *Immigrant* on each of our treatment conditions, we find that relative to the control, information alleging that Latinos undermine the quality of immigration to the United States reliably unsettles Asian perceptions of what it means to be a respectable *Immigrant* (-0.076, $p < 0.027$, one-tailed). Thus, we obtain a similar negative treatment effect, just as we anticipated and just as we obtained in our previous experiment with Asian adults, although it is noticeably weaker in size compared to our online study. We will say more about this in the meta-analysis that follows, but for now, we note that this effect is independent of any other of our administered treatments.

For our purposes, the larger point is that we obtain yet another negative effect for our *Immigrant status threat* manipulation on our mediator of interest, perceptions of being a respectable *Immigrant*. And, with two studies in hand now that focus on Asian adults, we have the ability to appraise whether, and to what degree, this treatment effect is substantively meaningful and statistically precise *across* Studies 4 and 5 (cf. Goh et al. 2016; see also Craig and Richeson 2018; Hopkins et al. 2020). We therefore undertook another meta-analysis that enables us to evaluate this proposition. Using this approach, our best estimate here is that the *Immigrant status threat* treatments we administered to Asian participants generate a small, measurable effect that is statistically reliable. In particular, *Immigrant status threat* upsets Asian individuals' sense of being a superior *Immigrant* group by downgrading their perceptions of this category by one-fifth of a standard deviation ($d = -0.218$, s.e. $= 0.109$, $p < 0.05$, two-tailed), which is substantively meaningful and distinguishable from zero at conventional levels (Cohen 1992). We read this consistency in effect size and

Table 7 Re-assessing status threat's impact on
Asian individuals' perceptions of being respectable
immigrants (Study 5, Lab)

	Being an Immigrant (1)
Status threat	−0.076*
	(0.038)
American threat	−0.061
	(0.039)
Realistic threat	−0.005
	(0.038)
Constant	0.574*
	(0.027)

Note: Entries are OLS coefficients with standard errors
in parentheses. For each model, $n = 141$. $*p < 0.05$, one-
tailed.

improved precision as indicating that, going forward, there is further room for
strengthening the effects of status threat to Asian Americans: a proposition that
will require further attention to how Asian Americans experience threats to their
social position within America's racial hierarchy.

5 What Have We Learned and What Do We Do with These Lessons?

Our overriding goal in this Element has been to extend prior work on racial
hierarchy in order to develop a framework that can more clearly and crisply
anticipate the *political* reactions of people of color toward each other (Masuoka
and Junn 2013; Pérez 2021; Zou and Cheryan 2017). Our efforts have yielded
a perspective where the social position of one's racial or ethnic group motivates
the political reactions that non-Whites express toward other communities of
color. This motivation stems from a profound need to preserve, if not to
enhance, the relative advantage that one's racial or ethnic group enjoys with
respect to other people of color within America's racial order. Indeed, while it is
still true that all people of color are positioned in relative disadvantage with
respect to Whites, our theorizing and evidence suggest there is more nuance in
the exact locations of each community of color within this hierarchy. These
shades of difference matter for the types of political opinions that members of
non-White groups express. Alas, one major implication emanating from our
work is that politics is but one channel through which people of color (re-)assert

their more favorable rank within a complex racial order. Paradoxically, then, it follows that the efforts of people of color to bolster their unique social position within this hierarchy serves to maintain the very configuration that fuels inequities between groups.

Indeed, although our empirical focus has been on Latinos as *the* threatening out-group, the basic principles we have identified should extend to a different setting; for example, when the out-group in question is either African Americans or Asian Americans. In order to provide some evidence for this proposition, we draw on the 2012 American National Study – a benchmark survey of the US public with a substantial oversample of Latino respondents ($n = 1,009$). If you recall our theoretical discussion, Latinos' rank in the racial order is such that they are deemed relatively un-American *and* socially inferior with respect to other communities of color. Although the ANES does not contain items specifically designed to capture Latinos' perceptions of these axes, we proxy for them here with measures of American and Latino identity strength.[13] To be sure, identities are not the same thing as perceptions of each axis in the racial order (Leach et al. 2008), but each identity should arguably be correlated with each dimension. By this reasoning, we treat these measures of *American* and *Latino* identity as loose gauges of Latino perceptions of each axis in the racial order. In turn, our outcomes are three policy proposals that address the well-being of African Americans: (1) federal aid to Blacks; (2) hiring equity for Blacks; and (3) and affirmative action for Blacks (scaled).[14]

Table 8 reports a basic correlational analysis where all variables are rescaled to range continuously from 0 to 1, with higher values indicating greater levels of identity and opposition to each policy proposal. Across each outcome, the evidence is unmistakably clear. The more invested Latinos are in their *American* identity, the more opposed they are to each policy proposal centering on African Americans. This makes sense since the (un)American dimension is one that is loosely shared with Black individuals – a relatively more American

---

[13] American identity: "How important is being American to your identity?", answered on 1–5 scale. Latino identity: "How important is being Hispanic to your identity?", also answered on 1–5 scale.

[14] Fair employment: "Should the government in Washington see to it that black people get fair treatment in jobs or is this not the federal government's business?", answered on 1–5 scale. Affirmative action: "Do you favor, oppose, or neither favor nor oppose allowing companies to increase the number of black workers by considering race along with other factors when choosing employees?" "Do you favor, oppose, or neither favor nor oppose allowing universities to increase the number of black students studying at their schools by considering race along with other factors when choosing students?" Both of these items were answered on 1 to 7 scales. Federal aid: "Where would you place yourself on this scale, or haven't you thought much about this?", with response options from 1-Government should help Blacks to 7-Blacks should help themselves.

Table 8 Latinos' location in racial order associated with attitudes toward Blacks

	Oppose job equity (Blacks)	Oppose federal aid (Blacks)	Oppose affirmative action (Blacks)
American	0.211*	0.192*	0.157*
ID	(0.059)	(0.045)	(0.035)
Latino ID	–0.263*	–0.212*	–0.181*
	(0.052)	(0.037)	(0.030)
Constant	0.512*	0.562*	0.589*
	(0.053)	(0.041)	(0.032)
N	828	754	890

Note: Source is the 2012 ANES. Latino respondents only. $*p < 0.05$, two-tailed.

group. In turn, the more invested Latinos are in their pan-ethnic identity, the *less* opposed they are to Black-centered policies. This pattern also makes theoretical sense, since the inferiority dimension is one shared by both Latinos *and* Blacks. In short, this provisional evidence underlines the viability of our approach to other communities of color within America's racial order.

Besides the general feasibility of our proposed framework, we also believe that another main contribution of this Element is its development of a theoretical framework that is conceptually unified, which allows us to use the same moving parts to explain the politics of various communities of color. We see this as a major breakthrough in a field that leans more heavily toward highly specialized theories that are limited to specific non-White groups (Dawson 1994; Kuo et al. 2017; Zepeda-Millan 2017). In saying this, we do not mean to imply that such work is useless, unappreciated, or irrelevant. Quite the contrary, we believe that in a diversifying polity like the United States, this research is profoundly essential to efforts at conceptually accommodating the unique, granular experiences of distinct peoples of color under common explanatory banners. In our mind, this can better position REP scholars to more fully appreciate the "forest" from the "trees" in producing knowledge about non-Whites, thus equipping us to yield more widely generalizable insights about current groups and others like them in the future.

We also wish to point out that our striving for more generalizable knowledge in a complex setting like US race relations holds implications for those working in highly heterogeneous settings like it. In this way, REP scholars can teach non-specialists a thing or two about conducting social science in highly diverse contexts, especially when these efforts entail (re)conceptualization (Adcock and Collier 2001; Collier and Mahon 1993; Sartori 1970). Let us say a bit more about what we mean here.

Any time that scholars face the prospect of developing concepts that apply to and travel across units – here, various people of color – a sense of unease and dread is not entirely unreasonable. Why? Because these steady efforts at generating new, broadly applicable concepts are difficult, time-consuming, and fraught with trial-and-error. Consider the usual trajectory of any concept, such as racial hierarchy. Typically, a scholar or set of scholars develops said concept with a limited set of cases in mind. In the case of America's racial order, this primarily occurred through the lens of Black-White relations (Carter and Pérez 2016; Sidanius et al. 1997; Sidanius and Pratto 1999).

As the research program around a concept, like racial hierarchy, begins to expand, researchers often feel real pressure to broaden and fan out this initial concept to cover new empirical terrain. In the instance of America's hierarchy, this has included efforts to integrate new groups into the conventional wisdom, such as Asian Americans, Latinos, Native Americans, and others who do not quite fit the original binary framework centered around Blacks and Whites (Abrajano and Alvarez 2010; Garcia 2012; Junn 2007; Kim 2003; Lien et al. 2004; Mora 2014; Wong et al. 2011). This process has involved stretching the original concept of a top-down hierarchy to the point that it might undermine the original coherence it served (Adcock and Collier 2001; Collier and Mahon 1993; Sartori 1970).

When faced with these types of circumstances, Giovanni Sartori (1970) long ago taught us that it is useful to think of concepts as straddling two dimensions: *extension* and *intension*. Whereas *extension* comprises the empirical entities that a concept refers to (e.g., units), *intension* refers to the attributes or meanings that merit a conceptual label. Simultaneously increasing the *extension* and *intension* of racial hierarchy in the United States is what, we think, our proposed framework accomplishes in spirit. That is, insofar as *extension* is concerned, the previous pages suggest an expanded sense of hierarchy that operates, not only in vertical fashion through the widely familiar *superior-inferior* dimension highlighted by prior work (Carter and Pérez 2016; Sidanius et al. 1997), but also horizontally in terms of a much-less-appreciated *American-foreign* dimension (Zou and Cheryan 2017). This enables us to credibly stretch the concept of racial hierarchy to accommodate and explain the political attitudes of multiple communities of color.

In covering and justifying the expansion of this terrain of racial groups, we have also clarified and made more precise the *intension* of racial hierarchy in the United States. This can be seen in our efforts to extend thinking about the position of people of color as running alongside two corridors, rather than just one (Zou and Cheryan 2017). In this view, all groups (Whites included) can be located on a *superior-inferior* axis, as well as an *American-foreign* axis. The fuller integration of this latter plane better accommodates varied racial groups and their experiences in the United States, while enabling scholars to better isolate some of the core causes of their continued subjugation in America. This is not to suggest that in light of our evidence, our knowledge of intergroup politics is complete or sufficient. But it is to say that our grasp of intergroup relations is more comprehensive than it was before.

In order to better appreciate this, compare prior knowledge about US Black-Latino relations in light of the reconceptualization we are advocating for (e.g., McClain and Karnig 1990; McClain et al. 2005; Sniderman and Piazza 2002). In the absence of our findings, research on these two groups generally construes their interactions as stemming from deep-seated prejudices that are magnified by zero-sum competition in politics, the economy, and other domains (Gay 2006). Here, if the world that Latinos and African Americans inhabit is a competitive jungle, then the material pressures they experience facilitates the expression of negative sentiments and views they already personally hold toward each other.

There is an intuitive ring to this characterization. Yet from a scientific perspective, we believe it is too individualistic an account and overly focused on people's views of the out-group. Indeed, if you pay closer attention here to details, you will find that a major implication of previous work is that personal dislike of out-groups – aided and abetted by material deprivation – is what drives intergroup conflict. The solution, then, would seem to be injecting greater parity into domains where competition exists. Surely, Black-Latino relations would improve then, right?

Perhaps. But it would not eliminate tensions between these groups, since the nature and sources of their shared frictions are somewhat misdiagnosed. Indeed, if prior work focuses on relative deprivation and personal attitudes toward others as the main levers to explain intergroup conflict, then our framework trains our attention on *in-group dynamics* and *social positioning* as key moving parts in the nature of intergroup politics. According to our account, Blacks and Latinos can live in a world where they have positive attitudes toward each other's group, sense no competition toward each other, and yet still experience tense relations. And the reason for this, our findings suggest, is because so much of intergroup relations is focused on the in-group – that is, one's own group – and the concerns about status and prestige revolving around it (Brewer 1999; Tajfel 1981; Turner et al. 1987).

Still not convinced? Then consider what our results suggest about Asian-Latino relations. Here are two groups that generally do not share the same labor markets, the same neighborhoods, or the same schools – in short, hardly any material conflicts exist between them. And yet, our framework predicts that these groups will sometimes still have conflictual political relations, not because of how they feel toward each other, but because of how concerned they are about the social position of their own in-group. Indeed, in our analysis of Asian-Latino relations, we established that when Asian Americans' sense of being a more *superior* community of color is undermined, they express greater intolerance toward Latinos as a way to reassert the perceived loss in social prestige of their own group.

Of course, in outlining what our framework has to say about the sources and functions of intergroup *conflict*, we do not mean to imply that our perspective is useful only in explaining why tensions sometimes explode between non-White groups. Alas, we think that going forward, our results have plenty of implications for the prospect of political *cooperation* between sundry minority groups. And this ideal can be accomplished, we believe, by availing ourselves of the same two axes that yielded the insights we have reported so far. This is how.

In our view of things, distinct groups of color can display hostility toward others out of a self-centered concern for the status and prestige of one's in-group. Here, one's outlook is focused on where one's in-group is socially located and with respect to whom. Indeed, we have gone to great lengths to demonstrate how, in relative terms, each group in America's racial order is uniquely positioned with respect to others. But one hidden benefit of this more nuanced hierarchy is that multiple groups often *share* space along a common dimension, thus highlighting a major psychological principle for developing and sustaining coalitions among people of color. By this view, various communities of color can be collectively galvanized toward political ends by underscoring the experiences, characteristics, and perspectives that tether them to a common plane in the racial order (Pérez 2020, 2021). For example, Asian Americans are stereotyped as more *superior* than African Americans and Latinos. But it is also the case that Asian Americans and Latinos are comparably stereotyped as more *foreign* than are African Americans. Greater unity can therefore be achieved, in principle, among some Asian Americans, Latinos, and even some African Americans (e.g., Caribbean immigrants) by training their focus on those aspects of politics – institutions, elites, norms – that keep them, collectively, at a disadvantage on the basis of their alleged *foreignness* (e.g., Craig et al. n.d.). In a similar vein, although Black individuals are stereotyped as a more *American* group than Asians and Latinos, it is also the case that African Americans and Latinos occupy a similar space as relatively *inferior* groups, especially when compared to Asian Americans. Accordingly, greater cohesion and cooperation can be attained, in principle, among African Americans, Latinos, and some Asian Americans (e.g., Hmong) by directing their attention to the political sources of their shared disadvantage as socially *inferior* communities. We point out all of this in order to stress that a more cooperative brand of politics between non-White groups can be produced, with some effort, by underlining the axis of subordination that a mix of groups shares. In fact, there are promising signs of this already, as evidenced by scholarship showing how a shared sense of disadvantage can lead members of non-White groups to unify and act politically as *people of color* (Cortland et al. 2017; Pérez 2020, 2021). Going forward, a major implication of our proposed framework is that several motivations and mechanisms, like those described here, exist for community activists, politicians, and other civic actors to build more sustainably cooperative relations between non-White individuals.

Before closing out this monograph, we wish to make one last point, and it concerns the prospects for changes in America's hierarchy. In expanding our understanding about how racial hierarchy works in the United States, we do not mean to imply that this order between groups is unyielding and unchanging. Yes, it is stable. But within its configuration lay some of the very keys to understanding when and how group positions change within this structure. In order to better isolate these conditions, we recommend reorienting our gaze away from the interaction *between* groups to the jockeying that takes place *within* groups. And here, at least two considerations should help to better anticipate transformations in America's racial order.

The first of these considerations involves the location of group members within a larger collective. Much like other phenomena in social life, groups can be characterized as distributions of members who possess a closed-set of attributes (Tajfel et al. 1971; Tajfel and Turner 1986; Turner et al. 1987; see also Chandra 2012). Within that distribution, there are *core* members who embody what a "real" group member looks and acts like. These are, formally speaking, prototypical members (cf. Danbold and Huo 2015; Schmitt and Branscombe 2001). But there are also *marginal* or peripheral members – individuals who occupy the edges of a group and are considered to be weaker reflections of the shared collective (Ellemers and Jetten 2013; Jetten et al. 2003).

Viewed from this angle, the distinctions between marginal and core members of a group vary in many ways, including their underlying motivations, particularly when a group's status is jeopardized. Marginal group members are especially sensitive to stimuli that undermine a group's status, prestige, or prospects; in particular, they are more likely to psychologically exit a group when it is possible (Ellemers et al. 2002; Jetten et al. 2003). When is this more likely? It is particularly likely when a group is not that important to a person's sense of self – that is, when a group is a weak reflection of how one thinks of oneself (Leach et al. 2008; Pérez 2015a, 2015b). This is the second consideration to heed when predicting transformations in the hierarchy. The less crucial a group is to a person's sense of self, and the more marginal one's location within that group, the more we should anticipate a person to bolt from the group when it is placed under stress (Ellemers and Jetten 2013; Jetten et al. 2003).

In the savanna of intergroup life that is America's hierarchy, our discussion here means that under some circumstances, a group's relative positioning can shift – gradually, but perceptibly – simply by the internal dynamics playing out between members of a shared group. As but one example, consider the transition of some Asian Americans and Latinos out of their respective racial or ethnic groups and into the "mainstream" – what some sociologists call immigrant assimilation (Alba and Nee 2003), but what we prefer to call incorporation.[15] As countless studies document, the stigmatization of Asian Americans and Latinos is often a psychological burden too heavy to bear. Consequently, some in-group members deal with their stigmatization by simply dissociating from the group, that is, by trading identification with the racial/ ethnic in-group for identification with a more positively esteemed group, racial or not (Garcia Bedolla 2005; Pérez 2015a, 2015b; Tajfel and Turner 1986).

For groups like Asian Americans and Latinos, who are stereotyped as being more *foreign* than others, the unfolding of intragroup dynamics along these lines suggests that internecine conflicts can sometimes produce a gradual softening of an in-group's stigmatization, as some members leave for the comfort and prestige of another out-group, like *Americans*. By the same token, those who are left behind are more likely to cling harder to their group, potentially reifying the very differences that feed their original social location. Yet what outsiders will observe are gradual adjustments in the social locations of these communities of color, with some Asian Americans and Latinos climbing in relative prestige, and others remaining in their original post.

In the end, whether America's racial order can be more fully upended is an empirical prediction that we cannot just rule out by fiat. But the panoramic expertise of REP scholars encourages all of us, ourselves included, to not lose hope and to be patient with how quickly and extensively deeper transformations in America's racial order occur over time. We cautiously, but optimistically, await these changes.

---

[15] Assimilation entails a homogenizing effect, where individuals cease being, say, Asian American or Latino, in exchange for becoming, say, American. Incorporation, in contrast, allows for the possibility of learning or acquiring a new identity (e.g., American identity), without necessarily giving up one's former attachment (e.g., ethnic identity) (e.g., Shih et al. 1999; Pérez et al. 2019).

Appendix
Racial Order, Racialized Responses

A.1 Control Group and Treatments: "Unsettled American" Experiment (Black Adults)

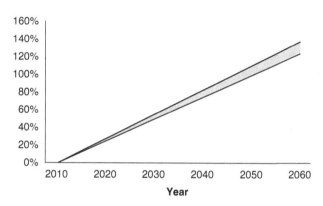

Figure 1A. Estimated % change in geographic mobility (2010–2060)

New US Census Bureau data suggest that the rate of geographical mobility, or the number of individuals who have moved within the past year, is increasing. The national mover rate increased from a record low of 11.6 percent in 2011 to 12.0 percent in 2012. According to the new data, about 36.5 million people changed residences in the United States within the past year. A majority (64.4 percent) of all movers stayed within the same county.

The estimates also reveal that many of the nation's fastest-growing communities are suburbs. For example, suburbs had 17.9 million move in and 9.2 million move out – an increase of 8.7 million movers. For those who moved to a different county or state, the reasons for moving varied considerably by the length of their move (e.g., family-related, job-related). "A greater amount of geographic mobility is now evident in all parts of the country – in large and small metropolitan areas, in the Snowbelt and in the Sunbelt," said Mark Gray, a demographer at the Brookings Institution, who analyzed the Census Bureau data.

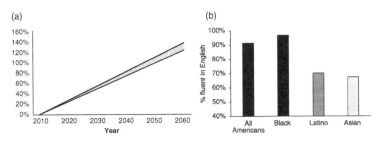

Figure 2A. a) Estimated % Latino population growth (2010–2060) b) English fluency in the US

New US Census Bureau data reveal that Latinos are a rapidly growing ethnic group, making it the largest of the three major ethnic minority populations in the United States (i.e., Asians, Latinos, and Blacks). According to Census Bureau data, the Latino population is expected to more than double in the next forty years, increasing four times faster than the total US population. A greater Latino presence in communities throughout the country is redefining what it means to be an American in major ways.

Indeed, in a community with a substantial Latino population, long-time resident Tyrone Washington said, "I used to think that being American was about speaking English, eating cheeseburgers, and following American politics. But when I see Latinos, I see people who live here in the United States, yet want to speak Spanish, eat *pozole* and *mondongo*, and follow their home country's politics. Unlike the rest of us, Latinos don't seem to be a part of the American way of life and are instead trying to transform the U.S. into their own culture and image."

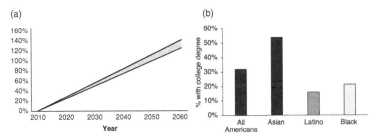

Figure 3A. a) Estimated % Latino population growth (2010–2060) b) College education levels in the US

New US Census Bureau data reveal that Latinos are a rapidly growing ethnic group, making it the largest of the three major ethnic minority populations in the United States (i.e., Asians, Latinos, and Blacks). According to Census Bureau data, the Latino population is expected to more than double in the next forty years, increasing four times faster than the total US population. A greater Latino presence in communities throughout the country is redefining what it means to be a respectable immigrant in major ways.

Indeed, in a community with a substantial Latino population, long-time resident Tyrone Washington said, "I used to think that being a good immigrant was about following this country's laws, providing for your own family, and sending your children to college. But when I see Latinos, I see people who break immigration laws, rely on food stamps to feed their family, and don't care about whether their children receive more than a high school education. Unlike the rest of us, Latinos are bringing down the quality of immigrants coming to and living in the United States."

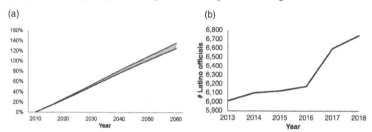

Figure 4A. a) Estimated % Latino population growth (2010–2020) b) Latino elected officials in the US

New US Census Bureau data reveal that Latinos are a rapidly growing ethnic group, making it the largest of the three major ethnic minority populations in the United States (i.e., Asians, Latinos, and Blacks). According to Census Bureau data, the Latino population is expected to more than double in the next forty years, increasing four times faster than the total US population. A greater Latino presence in communities throughout the country is redefining political representation for people in major ways.

Indeed, in a community with a substantial Latino population, long-time resident Tyrone Washington said, "I used to think that my political interests were well represented. But when I see Latinos, I see people who are quickly increasing their own group's political representation. Many Latinos are getting elected to positions of power in local, state, and national politics, which means less attention to the political issues that people like me deeply care about."

A.2 Raw Results from Structural Equation Model (SEM) – "Unsettled American" Experiment with Black Adults: Measurement Results

Table 1A. Measurement Results

	Loadings (standard errors)
American perceptions	
Important to be US-born	1.770* (0.100)
Important to live in USA for long time	1.548* (0.096)

Table 1A. (cont.)

	Loadings (standard errors)
Immigrant perceptions	
Important to have technical skills	1.612* (0.098)
Important to have higher education	1.801* (0.097)
Favorability toward people of color	
Favorability toward Blacks	1.275* (0.075)
Favorability toward Latinos	1.342* (0.060)
Favorability toward Asians	1.070* (0.054)
Opposition to immigration	
Increase time for citizenship	0.823* (0.081)
Decrease resources for arrests	0.878* (0.075)
Renew deportation relief	1.084* (0.066)
Provide pathway to citizenship	1.132* (0.064)
Pro-environmental attitudes	
Levy a green gas tax	1.108* (0.082)
Regulate carbon dioxide emissions	1.118* (0.071)
Raise threshold of fuel efficiency	0.911* (0.064)
Single items	
Establish English as official language	–
CFI/TLI	0.945/0.920
RMSEA [90% CI]	0.059 [0.050, 0.069]
N	409

Table 2A. Structural Results

	American perceptions	*Immigrant* Perceptions
American Threat	−0.482*	0.201
	(0.157)	(0.148)
Status Threat	−0.241	−0.162
	(0.157)	(0.151)
Realistic Condition	−0.338*	−0.145
	(0.156)	(0.147)

Table 3A. Structural Results

	Favorability toward PoC	Support English-only	Oppose immigration	Pro-environment
American	–0.195*	0.970*	0.413*	–0.090
perceptions	(0.069)	(0.115)	(0.081)	(0.075)
Immigrant	–0.142*	0.188	0.288*	–0.123
perceptions	(0.065)	(0.108)	(0.075)	(0.071)

Note: Model estimated via full information maximum likelihood (ML) in Mplus. All variables have a 1 to 7-point metric. $N = 409$ for both models. *$p < 0.05$, two-tailed.

A.3 Control Group and Treatments: "Unsettled Immigrant" Experiment (Asian Adults)

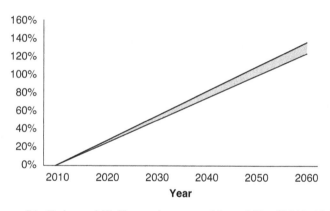

Figure 5A. Estimated % Change in geographic mobility (2010–2060)

New US Census Bureau data suggest that the rate of geographical mobility, or the number of individuals who have moved within the past year, is increasing. The national mover rate increased from a record low of 11.6 percent in 2011 to 12.0 percent in 2012. According to the new data, about 36.5 million people changed residences in the United States within the past year. A majority (64.4 percent) of all movers stayed within the same county.

The estimates also reveal that many of the nation's fastest-growing communities are suburbs. For example, suburbs had 17.9 million move in and 9.2 million move out – an increase of 8.7 million movers. For those who moved to a different county or state, the reasons for moving varied considerably by the length of their move (e.g., family-related, job-related). "A greater amount of geographic mobility is now evident in all parts of the country – in large and small metropolitan areas, in the Snowbelt and in the Sunbelt," said Mark Gray, a demographer at the Brookings Institution, who analyzed the Census Bureau data.

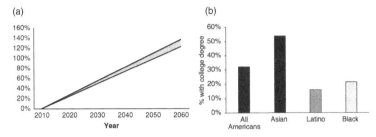

Figure 6A. a) Estimated % Latino population growth (2010–2060) b) College education levels in the US

New US Census Bureau data reveal that Latinos are a rapidly growing ethnic group, making it the largest of the three major ethnic minority populations in the United States (i.e., Asians, Latinos, and Blacks). According to Census Bureau data, the Latino population is expected to more than double in the next forty years, increasing four times faster than the total US population. A greater Latino presence in communities throughout the country is redefining what it means to be a respectable immigrant in major ways.

Indeed, in a community with a substantial Latino population, long-time resident Eric Hong said, "I used to think that being a good immigrant was about following this country's laws, providing for your own family, and sending your children to college. But when I see Latinos, I see people who break immigration laws, rely on food stamps to feed their family, and don't care about whether their children receive more than a high school education. Unlike the rest of us, Latinos are bringing down the quality of immigrants coming to and living in the United States."

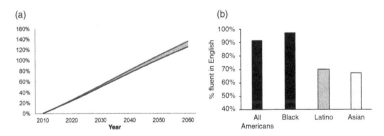

Figure 7A. a) Esimated % Latino population growth (2010–2060) b) English fluency in the US

New US Census Bureau data reveal that Latinos are a rapidly growing ethnic group, making it the largest of the three major ethnic minority populations in the United States (i.e., Asians, Latinos, and Blacks). According to

Census Bureau data, the Latino population is expected to more than double in the next forty years, increasing four times faster than the total US population. A greater Latino presence in communities throughout the country is redefining what it means to be an American in major ways.

Indeed, in a community with a substantial Latino population, long-time resident Eric Hong said, "I used to think that being American was about speaking English, eating cheeseburgers, and following American politics. But when I see Latinos, I see people who live here in the United States, yet want to speak Spanish, eat *pozole* and *mondongo*, and follow their home country's politics. Unlike the rest of us, Latinos don't seem to be a part of the American way of life and are instead trying to transform the United States into their own culture and image."

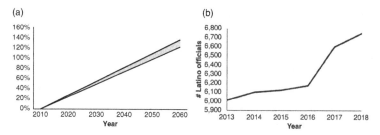

Figure 8A. a) Estimated % Latino population growth (2010–2060) b) Latino elected officials in the US

New US Census Bureau data reveal that Latinos are a rapidly growing ethnic group, making it the largest of the three major ethnic minority populations in the United States (i.e., Asians, Latinos, and Blacks). According to Census Bureau data, the Latino population is expected to more than double in the next forty years, increasing four times faster than the total US population. A greater Latino presence in communities throughout the country is redefining political representation for people in major ways.

Indeed, in a community with a substantial Latino population, long-time resident Eric Hong said, "I used to think that my political interests were well represented. But when I see Latinos, I see people who are quickly increasing their own group's political representation. Many Latinos are getting elected to positions of power in local, state, and national politics, which means less attention to the political issues that people like me deeply care about."

A.4 Raw Results from Structural Equation Model (SEM) – "Unsettled Immigrant" Experiment with Asian Adults

Table 4A. Measurement Results

	Loadings (standard errors)
American perceptions	
Important to be US-born	1.348* (0.112)
Important to live in USA for long time	1.340* (0.109)
Immigrant perceptions	
Important to have technical skills	1.441* (0.080)
Important to have higher education	1.479* (0.078)
Favorability toward people of color	
Favorability toward Blacks	1.160* (0.062)
Favorability toward Latinos	1.139* (0.056)
Favorability toward Asians	0.688* (0.060)
Opposition to immigration	
Increase time for citizenship	0.656* (0.073)
Decrease resources for arrests	0.826* (0.075)
Renew deportation relief	0.897* (0.062)
Provide pathway to citizenship	0.975* (0.065)
Pro-environmental attitudes	
Levy a green gas tax	1.127* (0.071)
Regulate carbon dioxide emissions	1.094* (0.062)
Raise threshold of fuel efficiency	0.909* (0.064)
Single items	
Establish English as official language	–
CFI/TLI	0.937/0.908
RMSEA [90% CI]	0.059 [0.050, 0.069]
N	405

Table 5A. Structural Results

	American perceptions	Immigrant Perceptions
Status Threat	0.079	−0.255^
	(0.163)	(0.149)
American Threat	0.130	0.049
	(0.164)	(0.149)
Realistic Condition	0.084	−0.051
	(0.164)	(0.149)

Table 6A. Structural Results

	Favorability toward PoC	Support English-only	Oppose immigration	Pro-environment
American	−0.130	0.478*	0.131	−0.171*
perceptions	(0.071)	(0.121)	(0.090)	(0.076)
Immigrant	−0.189*	0.344*	0.358*	−0.060
perceptions	(0.067)	(0.113)	(0.078)	(0.069)

Note: Model estimated via full information maximum likelihood (ML) in Mplus. All variables have a 1 to 7-point metric. $N = 409$ for both models. $*p<.05$, $^p<.10$, two-tailed.

References

Abrajano, Marisa A. 2010. *Campaigning to the New American Electorate*. Palo Alto: Stanford University Press.

Abrajano, Marisa A., and R. Michael Alvarez. 2010. *New Faces, New Voices: The Hispanic Electorate in America*. Princeton: Princeton University Press.

Abrajano, Marisa A., and Zoltan Hajnal. 2015. *White Backlash: Immigration, Race, and American Politics*. Princeton: Princeton University Press.

Acuña, Rodolfo. 1981. *Occupied America: A History of Chicanos*. New York: Harper & Row.

Adcock, Robert, and David Collier. 2001. Measurement Validity: A Shared Standard for Qualitative and Quantitative Research. *American Political Science Review* 95(3): 529–546.

Alba, Richard, and Victor Nee. 2003. *Remaking the American Mainstream: Assimilation and Contemporary Immigration*. Cambridge: Harvard University Press.

Baron, Reuben M., and David A. Kenny. 1986. The Moderator-Mediator Distinction in Social Psychological Research: Conceptual, Strategic, and Statistical Considerations. *Journal of Personality and Social Psychology* 51 (6): 1173–1182.

Barreto, Matt A. 2007. Si Se Puede! Latino Candidates and the Mobilization of Latino Voters. *American Political Science Review* 101(3): 425–441.

Beltrán, Cristina. 2010. *The Trouble with Unity: Latino Politics and the Creation of Identity*. New York: Oxford University Press.

Benjamin, Andrea. 2017. *Racial Coalition Building in Local Elections: Elite Cues and Cross-Ethnic Voting*. New York: Cambridge University Press.

Billig, Michael, and Henri Tajfel. 1973. Social Categorization and Similarity in Intergroup Behaviour. *European Journal of Social Psychology* 3(1): 27–52.

Block, Ray. 2011. What about Disillusionment? Exploring the Pathways to Black Nationalism. *Political Behavior* 33(1): 27–51.

Blum, Rachel Marie, and Christopher Sebastian Parker. 2019. Trump-ing Foreign Affairs: Status Threat and Foreign Policy Preferences on the Right. *Perspectives on Politics* 17(3): 737–755.

Blumer, Herbert. 1958. Race Prejudice as a Sense of Group Position. *Pacific Sociological Review* 1: 3–7.

Bobo, Lawrence, and Vincent L. Hutchings. 1996. Perceptions of Racial Group Competition: Extending Blumer's Theory of Group Position to a Multiracial Context. *American Sociological Review* 61(6): 951–972.

Bollen, Kenneth A. 1989. *Structural Equations with Latent Variables.* New York: Wiley.

Bonilla Silva, Eduardo. 2004. From Bi-Racial to Tri-Racial: Towards a New System of Racial Stratification in the USA. *Ethnic and Racial Studies* 6: 931–950.

Branscombe, Nyla R., Michael T. Schmitt, and Richard D. Harvey. 1999. Perceiving Pervasive Discrimination among African Americans: Implications for Group Identification and Well-Being. *Journal of Personality and Social Psychology* 77(1): 135–149.

Brewer, Marilynn B. 1999. The Psychology of Prejudice: Ingroup Love or Outgroup Hate? *Journal of Social Issues* 55(3): 429–444.

Brown, Ronald E., and Darren W. Davis. 2002. The Antipathy of Black Nationalism: Behavioral and Attitudinal Implications of an African American Ideology. *American Journal of Political Science* 46(2): 239–252.

Brown, Timothy A. 2007. *Confirmatory Factor Analysis for Applied Research.* New York: Guilford Press.

Cain, Bruce E., D. Roderick Kiwiet, and Carole J. Uhlaner. 1991. The Acquisition of Partisanship by Latinos and Asian Americans. *American Journal of Political Science* 35(2): 390–422.

Carter, Niambi M. 2019. *American while Black: African Americans, Immigration, and the Limits of Citizenship.* New York: Oxford University Press.

Carter, Niambi, and Efrén O. Pérez. 2016. Race and Nation: How Racial Hierarchy Shapes National Attachments. *Political Psychology* 37(4): 497–513.

Chandra, Kanchan. 2012. *Constructivist Theories of Ethnic Politics.* New York: Oxford University Press.

Citrin, Jack, Cara Wong, and Brian Duff. 2001. The Meaning of American National Identity. In R. D. Ashore, L. Jussim, and D. Wilder, eds., *Social Identity, Intergroup Conflict, and Conflict Reduction.* New York: Oxford University Press, pp. 71–100.

Citrin, Jack, Amy Lerman, Michael Murakami, and Kathryn Pearson. 2007. Testing Huntington: Is Hispanic Immigration a Threat to American Identity? *Perspectives on Politics* 5(1): 31–48.

Cohen, Jacob. 1992. A Power Primer. *Psychological Bulletin* 112(1): 155–159.

Collier, David, and James E. Mahon. 1993. Conceptual "Stretching" Revisited: Adapting Categories in Comparative Analysis. *American Political Science Review* 87(4): 845–855.

Cortez, David. 2017. Broken Mirrors: Identity, Duty, and Belonging in an Age of the New La(tinx) Migra. Dissertation. Cornell University.

Cortez, David. 2020. Latinxs in La Migra: Why They Join and Why it Matters. *Political Research Quarterly.*

Cortland, Clarissa, Maureen A. Craig, Jenessa R. Shapiro, Jennifer A. Richeson, Rebecca Neel, and Noah Goldstein. 2017. Solidarity through Shared Disadvantage: Highlighting Shared Experiences of Discrimination Improves Relations Between Stigmatized Groups. *Journal of Personality and Social Psychology* 113(4): 547–567.

Craig, Maureen A., and Jennifer A. Richeson. 2014. On the Precipice of a "Majority-Minority" Nation: Perceived Status Threat from the Racial Demographic Shift Affects White Americans' Political Ideology. *Psychological Science* 25(6): 1189–1197.

Craig, Maureen A., and Jennifer A. Richeson. 2018. Hispanic Population Growth Engenders Conservative Shift Among Non-Hispanic Racial Minorities. *Social Psychological and Personality Science* 9(4): 383–392.

Craig, Maureen A., Linda Zou, (Max) Hui Bai, and Michelle M. Lee. n.d. Stereotypes about Political Attitudes and Coalitions among U.S. Racial Groups: Implications for Strategic Political Decision-Making. Unpublished manuscript.

Cutaia Wilkinson, Betina. 2015. *Partners or Rivals? Power and Latino, Black, and White Relations in the Twenty-First Century.* Charlottesville: University of Virginia Press.

Danbold, Felix, and Yuen Huo. 2015. No Longer All-American? Whites' Defensive Reactions to their Numerical Decline. *Social Psychological and Personality Science* 6: 210–218.

Dawson, Michael C. 1994. *Behind the Mule: Race and Class in African American Politics.* Princeton: Princeton University Press.

Dawson, Michael C. 2000. Slowly Coming to Grips with the Effects of the American Racial Order on American Policy Preferences. In D. O. Sears, J. Sidanius, and L. Bobo, eds., *Racialized Politics: The Debate about Racism in America.* Chicago: University of Chicago Press, pp. 344–357.

Dawson, Michael C. 2001. *Black Visions: The Roots of Contemporary African-American Political Ideologies.* Chicago: University of Chicago Press.

Dawson, Michael C. 2011. *Not in Our Lifetimes: The Future of Black Politics.* Chicago: University of Chicago Press.

Devos, Thierry, and Mahzarin R. Banaji. 2005. American = White? *Journal of Personality and Social Psychology* 88(3): 447–466.

Diamond, J. 1998. African American Attitudes toward United States Immigration Policy. *International Migration Review* 32(2): 451–470.

DuBois, W. E. B. 1903. *The Souls of Black Folk.* New York: Penguin.

Ellemers, Naomi, and Jolanda Jetten. 2013. The Many Ways to be Marginal in a Group. *Personality and Social Psychology Review* 17(1): 3–21.

Ellemers, Naomi, Russell Spears, and Bertjan Doosje. 2002. Self and Social Identity. *Annual Review of Psychology* 53: 161–186.

Flores, Stella, Toby J. Park, Samantha L. Viano, and Vanessa M. Coca. 2017. State Policy and the Educational Outcomes of English Learner and Immigrant Students: Three Administrative Data Stories. *American Behavioral Scientist* 61(14): 1824–1844.

Franklin, John Hope. 1947. *From Slavery to Freedom: A History of Negro Americans*. New York: Alfred A. Knopf.

Fritz, Matthew S., and David P. MacKinnon. 2007. Required Sample Size to Detect the Mediated Effect. *Psychological Science* 18(3): 233–239.

Gaertner, Samuel L., John F. Dovidio, Mary C. Rust et al. 1999. Reducing Intergroup Bias: Elements of Intergroup Cooperation. *Journal of Personality and Social Psychology* 76(3): 388–402.

García, John A. 2012. *Latino Politics in America: Community, Culture, and Interests*. Lanham: Rowman & Littlefield Publishers.

Garcia Bedolla, Lisa. 2005. *Fluid Borders: Latino Power, Identity, and Politics in Los Angeles*. Berkeley: University of California Press.

Gay, Claudine. 2006. Seeing Difference: The Effect of Economic Disparity on Black Attitudes toward Latinos. *American Journal of Political Science* 50(4): 982–997.

Goh, Jin X., Judith A. Hall, and Robert Rosenthal. 2016. Mini-Meta Analysis of Your Own Studies: Some Arguments on Why and a Primer on How. *Social and Personality Psychology Compass* 10: 535–549.

Greer, Christina M. 2013. *Black Ethnics: Race, Immigration, and the Pursuit of the American Dream*. New York: Oxford University Press.

Gusfield, Joseph R. 1963. *Symbolic Crusade: Status Politics and the American Temperance Movement*. Urbana: University of Illinois Press.

Hajnal, Zoltan L., and Taeku Lee. 2012. *Why Americans Don't Join the Party: Race, Immigration, and the Failure (of Political Parties) to Engage the Electorate*. Princeton: Princeton University Press.

Harris-Lacewell, Melissa. 2004. *Barbershops, Bibles, and BET: Everyday Talk and Black Political Thought*. Princeton: Princeton University Press.

Higginbotham Brooks, Evelyn. 1993. *Righteous Discontent: The Women's Movement in the Black Baptist Church, 1880–1920*. Cambridge: Harvard University Press.

Hofstadter, Richard. 1965. *The Paranoid Style in American Politics and Other Essays*. Cambridge: Harvard University Press.

Hopkins, Daniel J., Cheryl R. Kaiser, Efrén O. Pérez, Sara Hagá, Corin Ramos, and Michael Zárate. 2020. *Journal of Experimental Political Science* 7(2): 112–136.

Ignatiev, Noel. 1995. *How the Irish Became White*. New York: Routledge.

Jacobson, Matthew Frye. 1998. *Whiteness of a Different Color: European Immigrants and the Alchemy of Race*. Cambridge: Harvard University Press.

Jardina, Ashley. 2019. *White Identity Politics*. New York: Cambridge University Press.

Jetten, Jolanda, Nyla R. Branscombe, Russell Spears, and Blake M. McKimmie. 2003. Predicting the Path of Peripherals. *Personality and Social Psychology Bulletin* 29: 130–140.

Jiménez, Tomás J. 2010. *Replenished Ethnicity: Mexican Americans, Immigration, and Identity*. Berkeley: University of California Press.

Jiménez, Tomás J. 2017. *The Other Side of Assimilation: How Immigrants Are Changing American Life*. Berkeley: University of California Press.

Jiménez, Tomás R. , and Adam L. Horowitz 2013. When White is Just Alright: How Immigrants Redefine Achievement and Reconfigure the Ethnoracial Hierarchy. *American Sociological Review* 78(5): 849–871.

Jost, John T., and Jost Liviatan. 2007. False Consciousness. In R. F. Baumeister and K. D. Vohs, eds., *Encyclopedia of Social Psychology*. Thousand Oaks, CA: Sage, pp. 100–103.

Junn, Jane. 2007. From Coolie to Model Minority: U.S. Immigration Policy and the Construction of Racial Identity. *DuBois Review* 4(2): 355–373.

Junn, Jane, and Natalie Masuoka. 2008. Asian American Identity: Shared Racial Status and Political Context. *Perspective on Politics* 6(4): 729–740.

Katz, Daniel. 1960. The Functional Approach to the Study of Attitudes. *Public Opinion Quarterly* 24: 163–204.

Kim, Claire Jean. 1999. The Racial Triangulation of Asian Americans. *Politics and Society* 27(1): 105–138.

Kim, Claire Jean. 2003. *Bitter Fruit: The Politics of Black-Korean Conflict in New York City*. New Haven, CT: Yale University Press.

King, Desmond. 2000. *Making Americans: Immigration and the Origins of the Diverse Democracy*. New York: Oxford University Press.

Kuo, Alexander, Neil Malhotra, and Cecilia Hyunjung Mo. 2017. Social Exclusion and Political Identity: The Case of Asian American Partisanship. *Journal of Politics* 79: 17–32.

Lajevardi, Nazita. 2020. *Outsiders at Home: The Politics of American Islamophobia*. Cambridge: Cambridge University Press.

Leach, Colin Wayne, Martjin van Zomeren, Sven Zebel et al. 2008. Group-Level Self-Definition and Self-Investment: A Hierarchical (Multicomponent) Model of In-Group Identification. *Journal of Personality and Social Psychology* 95(1): 144–165.

Lee Merseth, Julie. 2018. Race-ing Solidarity: Asian Americans and Support for Black Lives Matter. *Politics, Groups, and Identities* 6(3): 337–356.

Lee, Jennifer, and Frank D. Bean. 2010. *The Diversity Paradox: Immigration and the Color Line in 21st Century America.* New York: Russell Sage Foundation.

Lee, Jennifer, and Min Zhou. 2015. *The Asian American Achievement Paradox.* New York: Russell Sage Foundation.

Lee, Taeku. 2002. *Mobilizing Public Opinion: Black Insurgency and Racial Attitudes in the Civil Rights Era.* Chicago: University of Chicago Press.

Lee, Taeku. 2008. Race, Immigration, and the Identity-to-Politics Link. *Annual Review of Political Science* 11: 457–478.

Lien, Pei-te, M. Margaret Conway, and Janelle Wong. 2004. *The Politics of Asian Americans: Diversity and Community.* New York: Routledge Press.

Lowery, Brian S., Eric D. Knowles, and Miguel M. Unzueta. 2007. Framing Inequity Safely: Whites' Motivated Perceptions of Racial Privilege. *Personality and Social Psychology Bulletin* 33(9): 1237–1250.

Malhotra, Neil, Yotam Margalit, and Cecilia Hyungjung Mo. 2013. Economic Explanations for Opposition to Immigration: Distinguishing Between Prevalence and Conditional Impact. *American Journal of Political Science* 57(2): 391–410.

Mancilla-Martínez, Jeannette, and Jennifer Wallace Jacoby. 2018. The Influence of Risk Factors on Preschoolers' Spanish Vocabulary Development in the Context of Spanish Instruction. *Early Education and Development* 29(4): 563–580.

Marx, Anthony W. 1998. *Making Race and Nation: A Comparison of the United States, South Africa, and Brazil.* New York: Cambridge University Press.

Mason, Lilliana. 2018. *Uncivil Agreement: How Politics Became Our Identity.* Chicago: University of Chicago Press.

Masuoka, Natalie R., and Jane Junn. 2013. *The Politics of Belonging: Race, Public Opinion, and Immigration.* Chicago: University of Chicago Press.

McClain, Paula D., and Jessica D. Johnson Carew 2017. *"Can We All Get along?" Racial and Ethnic Minorities in American Politics.* New York: Westview Press.

McClain, Paula D., and Albert K. Karnig. 1990. Black and Hispanic Socioeconomic and Political Competition. *American Political Science Review* 84(2): 535–545.

McClain, Paula D., Niambi M. Carter, Victoria M. DeFrancesco Soto et al. 2005. Racial Distancing in a Southern City: Latino Immigrants' Views of Black Americans. *Journal of Politics* 68(3): 571–584.

McClain, Paula D., Monique L. Lyle, Niambi M. Carter et al. 2007. Black Americans and Latino Immigrants in a Southern City. *DuBois Review* 4(1): 97–117.

McClain, Paula D., Jessica D. Johnson Carew, Eugene Walton, Jr., and Candis S. Watts. 2009. Group Membership, Group Identity, and Group Consciousness: Measures of Racial Identity in American Politics? *Annual Review of Political Science* 12: 471–485.

Mora, G. Cristina. 2014. *Making Hispanics: How Activists, Bureaucrats, and Media Constructed a New American*. Chicago: University of Chicago Press.

Mutz, Diana C. 2018. Status Threat, Not Economic Hardship, Explains the 2016 Presidential Vote *Proceedings of the National Academy of Sciences* 115(19): 4330–4339.

Nagel, Joane. 1996. *American Indian Ethnic Renewal: Red Power and the Resurgence of Identity and Culture*. New York: Oxford University Press.

Nakanishi, Don T. 1991. The Next Swing Vote? Asian Pacific Americans and California Politics. In B. O. Jackson and M. B. Preston, eds., *Racial and Ethnic Politics in California*. Berkeley: IGS Press, pp. 25–54.

Ngai, Mae. 2004. *Impossible Subjects: Illegal Aliens and the Making of Modern America*. Princeton: Princeton University Press.

Omi, Michael, and Howard Winant. 1986. *Racial Formation in the United States: From the Sixties to the Nineties*. New York: Routledge Press.

Oskooii, Kassra. 2016. How Discrimination Impacts Sociopolitical Behavior: A Multidimensional Perspective. *Political Psychology* 37(5): 613–640.

Oskooii, Kassra A. R. 2020. Perceived Discrimination and Political Behavior. *British Journal of Political Science* 50(3): 867–892.

Pantoja, Adrian D., Ricardo Ramirez, and Gary M. Segura. 2001. Citizens by Choice, Voters by Necessity: Patterns in Political Mobilization by Naturalized Latinos. *Political Research Quarterly* 54(4): 729–750.

Parker, Christopher S. 2009. *Fighting for Democracy: Black Veterans and the Struggle against White Supremacy in the Postwar South*. Princeton: Princeton University Press.

Parker, Christopher Sebastian, and Matt A. Barreto. 2013. *Change They Can't Believe In: The Tea Party and Reactionary Politics in America*. Princeton: Princeton University Press.

Pérez, Efrén O. 2010. Explicit Evidence on the Import of Implicit Attitudes: The IAT and Immigration Policy Judgments. *Political Behavior* 32(4): 517–545.

Pérez, Efrén O. 2015a. Ricochet: How Elite Discourse Politicizes Racial and Ethnic Identities. *Political Behavior* 37(1): 155–180.

Pérez, Efrén O. 2015b. Xenophobic Rhetoric and Its Political Effects on Immigrants and Their Co-Ethnics. *American Journal of Political Science* 59(3): 549–564.

Pérez, Efrén O. 2016. *Unspoken Politics: Implicit Attitudes and Political Thinking.* New York: Cambridge University Press.

Pérez, Efrén O. 2020. "People of Color" are Protesting: Here's What You Need to Know about This New Identity. Washington Post (The Monkey Cage).

Pérez, Efrén O. 2021. *Diversity's Child: People of Color and the Politics of Identity.* Chicago: University of Chicago Press.

Pérez, Efrén O., and Marc J. Hetherington. 2014. Authoritarianism in Black and White: Testing the Cross-Racial Validity of the Child-Rearing Scale. *Political Analysis* 22: 398–412.

Pérez, Efrén O., Maggie Deichert, and Andrew M. Engelhardt. 2019. E Pluribus Unum? How Ethnic and National Identity Motivate Reactions to a Political Ideal. *Journal of Politics* 81(4): 1420–1433.

Philpot, Tasha S. 2017. *Conservative but Not Republican: The Paradox of Party Identification and Ideology among African Americans.* New York: Cambridge University Press.

Reny, Tyler T., and Matt A. Barreto. 2020. Xenophobia in the Time of Pandemic: Othering, Anti-Asian Attitudes, and COVID-19. Politics, Groups, and Identities. Latest Articles.

Rogers, Reuel. 2006. *Afro-Caribbean Immigrants and the Politics of Incorporation: Ethnicity, Exception, or Exit.* New York: Cambridge University Press.

Sakamoto, Arthur, Kimberly A. Goyette, and ChanHwan Kim. 2009. Socioeconomic Attainment of Asian Americans. *Annual Review of Sociology* 35: 255–276.

Sanchez, Gabriel R., and Natalie Masuoka. 2010. Brown-Utility Heuristic? The Presence and Contributing Factors of Linked Fate. *Hispanic Journal of Behavioral Sciences* 32(4): 519–531.

Sartori, Giovanni. 1970. Concept Misformation in Comparative Politics. *American Political Science Review* 64: 1033–1053.

Schmitt, Michael T., and Nyla R. Branscombe. 2001. The Good, the Bad, and the Manly: Threats to One's Prototypicality and Evaluations of Fellow In-Group Members. *Journal of Experimental Social Psychology* 37(6): 510–517.

Sears, David O., and Victoria Savalei. 2006. The Political Color Line in America: Many "Peoples of Color" or Black Exceptionalism. *Political Psychology* 27(6): 895–924.

Sears, David O. 2015. The American Color Line and Black Exceptionalism. In J. P. Forgas, K. Fiedler, and W. R. Crano, eds., *Social Psychology and Politics*. New York: Psychology Press, pp. 337–352.

Sherif, Muzafer, O. J. Harvey, B. Jack White, William R. Hood, and Carolyn W. Sherif. 1961. *The Robbers Cave Experiment: Intergroup Conflict and Cooperation*. Norman: University of Oklahoma Press.

Shih, Margaret, Todd L. Pittinsky, and Nalini Ambady. 1999. Stereotype Susceptibility: Identity Salience and Shifts in Quantitative Performance. *Psychological Science* 10(1): 80–83.

Shrout, Patrick E., and Niall Bolger. 2002. Mediation in Experimental and Nonexperimental Studies: New Procedures and Recommendations. *Psychological Methods* 7(4): 422–445.

Sidanius, Jim, Seymour Feshbach, Shana Levin, and Felicia Pratto. 1997. The Interface Between Ethnic and National Attachment: Ethnic Pluralism or Ethnic Dominance? *Public Opinion Quarterly* 61(1): 102–133.

Sidanius, Jim, and Felicia Pratto. 1999. *Social Dominance: An Intergroup Theory of Social Hierarchy and Oppression*. New York: Cambridge University Press.

Sidanius, James, and John R. Petrocik. 2001. Communal and National Identity in a Multiethnic State: A Comparison of Three Perspectives. In R. D. Ashmore, L. Jussim, and D. Wilder, eds., *Social Identity, Intergroup Conflict, and Conflict Reduction*. New York: Oxford University Press, 101–127.

Silber Mohamed, Heather. 2017. *The New Americans? Immigration, Protest, and the Politics of Latino Identity*. Lawrence: University Press of Kansas.

Sirin, Cigdem V., Nicholas A. Valentino, and José D. Villalobos. 2016. Group Empathy in Response to Nonverbal Racial/Ethnic Cues: A National Experiment on Immigration Policy Attitudes. *American Behavioral Scientist* 60(14): 1676–1697.

Sniderman, Paul M., and Thomas Piazza. 2002. *Black Pride and Black Prejudice*. Princeton: Princeton University Press.

Sue, Stanley, and Sumie Okazaki. 1990. Asian American Educational Achievements: A Phenomenon in Search of an Explanation. *American Psychologist* 45(8): 913–920.

Tajfel, Henri. 1981. *Human Groups and Social Categories: Studies in Social Psychology*. New York: Cambridge University Press.

Tajfel, Henri, and John C. Turner. 1986. The Social Identity Theory of Intergroup Behavior. In W. G. Austin and S. Worchel, eds., *Psychology of Intergroup Relations*. Chicago: Hall Publishers, 7–24.

Tajfel, Henri, M. G. Billig, R. P. Bundy, and Claude Flament. 1971. Social Categorization and Intergroup Behaviour. *European Journal of Social Psychology* 1(2): 149–178.

Takaki, Ronald. 1989. *Strangers from Different Shores: A History of Asian Americans*. Boston: Little, Brown, and Company.

Tam Cho, Wendy. 1995. Asians – A Monolithic Voting Bloc? *Political Behavior* 17: 223–49.

Tate, Katherine. 1991. Black Political Participation in the 1984 and 1988 Presidential Elections. *American Political Science Review* 85(4): 1159–1176.

Tate, Katherine. 2000. *Black Faces in the Mirror: African Americans and Their Representatives in Congress*. Princeton: Princeton University Press.

Tavits, Margit, and Efrén O. Pérez 2019. Language Influences Mass Opinion toward Gender and LGBTQ Equality. *Proceedings of the National Academy of Sciences* 116(34): 16781–16786.

Telles, Edward, and Vilma Ortiz. 2008. *Generations of Exclusion: Mexican-Americans, Assimilation, and Race*. New York: Russell Sage Foundation.

Telles, Edward, and Christina A. Sue. 2019. *Durable Ethnicity: Mexican Americans and the Ethnic Core*. New York: Oxford University Press.

Telles, Edward, Mark Sawyer, and Gaspar Rivera-Salgado. 2011. *Just Neighbors? Research on African American and Latino Relations in the United States*. New York: Russell Sage Foundation.

Transue, John E. 2007. Identity Salience, Identity Acceptance, and Racial Policy Attitudes: American Identity as a Uniting Force. *American Journal of Political Science* 51(1): 78–91.

Tseng, Vivian, Ruth K. Chao, and Inna Artai Padmawidjaja. 2007. Asian Americans' Educational Experiences. In F. T. L. Leong, A. Ebreo, L. Kinoshita, A. G. Inman, and L. H., eds., *Handbook of Asian American Psychology*. Thousand Oaks: Sage Publications, pp. 105–123.

Tuan, Mia. 1998. *Forever Foreigners or Honorary Whites? The Asian Ethnic Experience Today*. New Brunswick: Rutgers University Press.

Tuan, Mia. 1998. *Forever Foreigners or Honorary Whites: The Asian Ethnic Experience Today*. New Brunswick: Rutgers University Press.

Turner, John C., Michael A. Hogg, Penelope J. Oakes, Stephen D. Reicher, and Margaret S. Wetherell. 1987. *Rediscovering the Social Group: A Self-Categorization Theory*. New York: Basil Blackwell.

Vaca, Nicolas. 2004. *The Presumed Alliance: The Unspoken Conflict Between Latinos and Blacks and What it Means for America*. New York: Rayo.

Vidal-Ortiz, Salvador. 2008. People of color. In R. T., Schaefer, ed., *Encyclopedia of Race, Ethnicity, and Society*. Thousand Oaks, CA: Sage Publications, pp. 103–107.

Waldzus, Sven, Amélie Mummendey, Michael Wenzel, and Franziska Boettcher. 2004. Of Bikers, Teachers, and Germans: Groups'

Diverging Views about their Prototypicality. *British Journal of Social Psychology* 43: 385–400.

Watts Smith, Candis. 2014. *Black Mosaic: The Politics of Black Pan-Ethnicity.* New York: NYU Press.

Wenzel, Michael, Amélie Mummendey, and Sven Waldzus. 2007. Superordinate Identities and Intergroup Conflict: The Ingroup Projection Model. *European Review of Social Psychology* 18(1): 331–372.

White, Ismail K. 2007. When Race Matters and When It Doesn't: Racial Group Differences in Response to Racial Cues. American Political Science Review 101(2): 339–354.

White, Ismail K., and Chryl N. Laird. 2020. *Steadfast Democrats: How Social Forces Shape Black Political Behavior.* Princeton: Princeton University Press.

White, Ismail K., Chryl N. Laird, and Troy D. Allen. 2014. Selling Out? The Politics of Navigating Conflicts Between Racial Group Interest and Self-Interest. *American Political Science Review* 108(4): 783–800.

Wong, Janelle. 2005. Mobilizing Asian American Voters: A Field Experiment. *Annals of the American Academy of Political and Social Science* 601(1): 102–114.

Wong, Janelle, S. Karthick Ramakrishnan, Taeku Lee, and Jane Junn. 2011. *Asian American Political Participation: Emerging Constituents and Their Political Identities.* New York: Russell Sage Foundation.

Xu, Jun, and Jennifer C. Lee. 2013. The Marginalized "Model" Minority: An Empirical Examination of the Racial Triangulation of Asian Americans. *Social Forces* 91: 1363–1397.

Zepeda-Millán, Chris. 2017. *Latino Mass Mobilization: Immigration, Racialization, and Activism.* New York: Cambridge University Press.

Zhao, Xinshu, John G. Lynch, Jr., and Qimi Chen. 2010. Reconsidering Baron and Kenny: Myths and Truths about Mediation Analysis. *Journal of Consumer Research* 37: 197–206.

Zou, Linda X., and Sapna Cheryan. 2017. Two Axes of Subordination: A New Model of Racial Position. *Journal of Personality and Social Psychology* 112 (5): 696–717.

Cambridge Elements ☰

Race, Ethnicity, and Politics

Megan Ming Francis
University of Washington

Megan Ming Francis is the G. Alan and Barbara Delsman Associate Professor of Political Science at the University of Washington and a Fellow at the Ash Center for Democratic Governance and the Carr Center for Human Rights at the Harvard Kennedy School. Francis is the author of the award winning book, *Civil Rights and the Making of the Modern American State*. She is particularly interested in American political and constitutional development, social movements, the criminal punishment system, Black politics, philanthropy, and the post–Civil War South.

About the Series

Elements in Race, Ethnicity, and Politics is an innovative publishing initiative in the social sciences. The series publishes important original research that breaks new ground in the study of race, ethnicity, and politics. It welcomes research that speaks to the current political moment, research that provides new perspectives on established debates, and interdisciplinary research that sheds new light on previously understudied topics and groups.

Cambridge Elements ☰

Race, Ethnicity, and Politics

Elements in the Series

Printed in the United States
by Baker & Taylor Publisher Services